# CAMBRIDGE LIBRARY COLLECTION

*Books of enduring scholarly value*

## Religion

For centuries, scripture and theology were the focus of prodigious amounts of scholarship and publishing, dominated in the English-speaking world by the work of Protestant Christians. Enlightenment philosophy and science, anthropology, ethnology and the colonial experience all brought new perspectives, lively debates and heated controversies to the study of religion and its role in the world, many of which continue to this day. This series explores the editing and interpretation of religious texts, the history of religious ideas and institutions, and not least the encounter between religion and science.

## Apocrypha Sinaitica

The sisters Agnes Lewis (1843–1926) and Margaret Gibson (1843–1920) were pioneering biblical scholars who became experts in a number of ancient languages. Travelling widely in the Middle East, they made several significant discoveries, including one of the earliest manuscripts of the Four Gospels in Syriac, a dialect of Aramaic, the language probably spoken by Jesus himself. Their chief discoveries were made in the Monastery of St. Catherine on Mount Sinai. This work is based on a manuscript discovered in the monastery in 1895 and first published in 1896. Originally published as part of the Studia Sinaitica, this fascicule comprises Arabic and Syriac texts of various apocryphal stories edited and translated by Margaret Gibson. The first part of the text contains the 'Anaphora Pilati', the story of the aftermath of Pontius Pilate's decision to crucify Jesus. Also included are the Clementine Recognitions and the Martyrdom of James and Simon.

Cambridge University Press has long been a pioneer in the reissuing of out-of-print titles from its own backlist, producing digital reprints of books that are still sought after by scholars and students but could not be reprinted economically using traditional technology. The Cambridge Library Collection extends this activity to a wider range of books which are still of importance to researchers and professionals, either for the source material they contain, or as landmarks in the history of their academic discipline.

Drawing from the world-renowned collections in the Cambridge University Library and other partner libraries, and guided by the advice of experts in each subject area, Cambridge University Press is using state-of-the-art scanning machines in its own Printing House to capture the content of each book selected for inclusion. The files are processed to give a consistently clear, crisp image, and the books finished to the high quality standard for which the Press is recognised around the world. The latest print-on-demand technology ensures that the books will remain available indefinitely, and that orders for single or multiple copies can quickly be supplied.

The Cambridge Library Collection brings back to life books of enduring scholarly value (including out-of-copyright works originally issued by other publishers) across a wide range of disciplines in the humanities and social sciences and in science and technology.

# Apocrypha Sinaitica

Edited and translated by
Margaret Dunlop Gibson

CAMBRIDGE UNIVERSITY PRESS

Cambridge, New York, Melbourne, Madrid, Cape Town,
Singapore, São Paolo, Delhi, Mexico City

Published in the United States of America by Cambridge University Press, New York

www.cambridge.org
Information on this title: www.cambridge.org/9781108043465

© in this compilation Cambridge University Press 2012

This edition first published 1896
This digitally printed version 2012

ISBN 978-1-108-04346-5 Paperback

# APOCRYPHA SINAITICA.

𝕷onȡon: C. J. CLAY AND SONS,
CAMBRIDGE UNIVERSITY PRESS WAREHOUSE,
AVE MARIA LANE.
𝕲lasgoⱳ: 263, ARGYLE STREET.

𝕷eipȝig: F. A. BROCKHAUS.
𝕹eⱳ 𝔜ork: MACMILLAN AND CO.

ANAPHORA PILATI. From No. 445.
(*From a photograph by M. D. Gibson.*)

*Frontispiece*

# STUDIA SINAITICA No. V.

# APOCRYPHA SINAITICA.

*EDITED AND TRANSLATED INTO ENGLISH*

BY

MARGARET DUNLOP GIBSON, M.R.A.S.

LONDON:
C. J. CLAY AND SONS,
CAMBRIDGE UNIVERSITY PRESS WAREHOUSE,
AVE MARIA LANE.
1896

𝕮𝖆𝖒𝖇𝖗𝖎𝖉𝖌𝖊 :

PRINTED BY J. AND C. F. CLAY

AT THE UNIVERSITY PRESS.

# CONTENTS.

## TEXTS.

## TRANSLATIONS.

A. P. *b*

## ILLUSTRATIONS.

# INTRODUCTION.

## ANAPHORA PILATI.

THE Anaphora Pilati, with its sequel, the Paradosis Pilati, has been edited by Tischendorf (*Evangelia Apocrypha*, Leipzig, 1876) from various Greek MSS., of dates ranging from the 12th to the 15th centuries. The Anaphora, in Greek, had been previously edited by J. A. Fabricius (*Cod. Apoc.* Vol. II. Hamburg, 1719), with a Latin version, and together with the Paradosis, by Birch (*Auctarium Cod. Apoc.* Copenhagen, 1804) and by Thilo (*Cod. Apoc. N.T.* Leipzig, 1832).

They are both usually found as a sequel to the Acta Pilati, and the Letters of Pilate and Herod.

We have not yet sufficient documentary evidence to determine either the time or place of production of any of these legends, though they seem to be connected with Edessa. There are traces of Pilate literature in Justin Martyr (A.D. 150), who says:

Apologia, I. 35. Καὶ ταῦτα ὅτι γέγονε, δύνασθε μαθεῖν ἐκ τῶν ἐπὶ Ποντίου Πιλάτου γενομένων ἄκτων.

Apol. I. 48. Ὅτι δὲ καὶ θεραπεύσειν πάσας νόσους καὶ νεκροὺς ἀνεγερεῖν ὁ ἡμέτερος Χριστὸς προεφητεύθη, ἀκούσατε τῶν λελεγμένων. Ἔστι δὲ ταῦτα· Τῇ παρουσίᾳ αὐτοῦ ἁλεῖται χωλὸς ὡς ἔλαφος, καὶ τρανὴ ἔσται γλῶσσα μογιλάλων· τυφλοὶ ἀναβλέψουσι, καὶ λεπροὶ καθαρισθήσονται, καὶ νεκροὶ ἀναστήσονται καὶ περιπατήσουσιν. Ὅτι τε ταῦτα ἐποίησεν, ἐκ τῶν ἐπὶ Ποντίου Πιλάτου γενομένων αὐτῷ μαθεῖν δύνασθε.

Tertullian (A.D. 150–220) says :

Apologeticus, c. 21. "Ea omnia super Christo Pilatus, et ipse iam pro sua conscientia Christianus, Caesari tunc Tiberio nuntiavit." Here a written document is assumed, but it may be only an inference from the language of Justin.

In the Syriac sermon of Simon Cepha (Cureton, *Ancient Syriac Documents*) we read, with an evident appeal to extant documents,

[Syriac text, 14 lines]

*Translation* (Cureton, p. 38). "And inasmuch as ye saw the sun become darkened at his death, ye yourselves also are witnesses. But the earth shook when he was slain, and the vail was rent at his death; and touching these things the Governor Pilate also was witness, for he sent and made them known to Caesar, and these things, and more than these, were read before him and before the princes of your city. And on this account Caesar was angry against Pilate, because he had unjustly been persuaded by the Jews, and for this reason he sent and took away from him the authority which he had given to him. And this same thing was published abroad and made known in all the dominion of the Romans. What therefore Pilate saw and made known to Caesar and to your honourable Senate, the same I preach and declare, and my fellow Apostles. And ye know that Pilate could not have written to the Government anything which did not take place and he saw with his own eyes: but that which did take place and was done in reality, the same he wrote and made known."

Lipsius, who has made a thorough examination of the subject, does not allow that the Acta Pilati and their sequels go back to an earlier date than the end of the fourth century. Tischendorf, on the other hand, believed them to go back to the second, and his opinion is supported by that of M. Nicolas (*Études sur les Évangiles Apocryphes*, pp. 360, 361). Even Lipsius's remarks, however, apply chiefly to the Acta, and he is inclined to give an earlier date to the Anaphora. He allows that magical ideas were rife among the Christians of the second century, and that it would be quite natural for them to imagine that the Roman idols fell down literally, as they did metaphorically, at the name of Jesus. He points out a trace of Marcionite ideas in the liberation of spirits from Hades, though he also says that this is counterbalanced by the said liberation being limited to patriarchs and prophets, instead of being extended to Old Testament evil-doers as well.

The Anaphora corresponds better with the documents mentioned by Justin than the Acta do, and better still with those mentioned by Tertullian. It has a rival for that honour in the shape of a letter from Pilate to Claudius, embedded in the Acta Petri et Pauli. It is evident, however, that our Lord suffered in the time of Tiberius.

Eusebius mentions heathen Acta Pilati (*Eccl. Hist.* Book I. c. 9, and IX. c. 5) but does not seem to know anything of Christian ones. He says that Maximin ordered these Acta, which were full of blasphemies against Christ, to be taught to the school children of every city and nation. Lipsius supposes that the Christian Acta were got up in opposition to these heathen ones, and are therefore of later date than Eusebius; but it is quite possible that they have a contrary relationship to one another.

The recent discovery of the pseudo-Gospel of Peter throws a corroborative light on some of the statements in the Anaphora. For example:

Ev. Petri, c. 5. Περιήρχοντο δὲ πολλοὶ μετὰ λύχνων νομίζοντες ὅτι νύξ ἐστιν.

Anaph. Pilati (Tischendorf, Ev. Apoc. rec. B.). Ἐν παντὶ τῷ κόσμῳ, ἦψαν λύχνους ἀπὸ ἕκτης ὥρας ἕως ὀψίας.

This is, however, absent from both our Syriac and Arabic recensions.

Ev. Petri, c. 10. τῶν μὲν δύο τὴν κεφαλὴν χωροῦσαν μέχρι τοῦ οὐρανοῦ.

Anaph. Pilati (Tisch. r. A.). Ἄνδρες ἐφαίνοντο ὑψηλοί.

Syriac, page ܡ, lines 9, 10. ܘܚܠܝܐ ܗܘܘ ܚܕܒܫܪܝܢ ܠܬܪܝܢ ܕܪܝܫܗܘܢ ܡܛܐ ܗܘܘ ܘܪܝܫܗ ܕܡܘܚܗ܂

Arabic, pp. ٤, ٥, l. 19. كذلك ظهروا رجال عظما بلباس بهى

Ev. Petri, c. 9. Μεγάλη φωνὴ ἐγένετο ἐν τῷ οὐρανῷ.

Anaph. Pilati (Tisch. r. A.). ἦχος ἐγένετο ἐκ τοῦ οὐρανοῦ.

Syriac, p. ܡ, ll. 12, 13. ܘܚܠܝܐ ܩܠܐ ܗܘܐ ܩܠܡ ܟܕ ܚܦܡ ܗܘܘ. ܐܝܟ ܘܠܐ ܕܒܪܝܐ ܪܐܝ܂

Arabic, pp. ٤, ٥, ll. 16, 17. صرخ صوت من السما

Ev. Petri, c. 10. Ἐκήρυξας τοῖς κοιμωμένοις;

Anaph. Pilati (Tisch. r. A.). Ἀνέλθατε ἐξ ᾅδου οἱ δεδουλωμένοι ἐν τοῖς καταχθονίοις τοῦ ᾅδου.

Syriac, p. ܗ, ll. 15, 16. ܗܘܘ ܠܘܬ ܐܝܠܝܢ ܕܫܒܝܢ ܗܘܘ ܒܥܘ̈ܡܩܐ ܬܚܬܝ̈ܬܐ ܕܫܝܘܠ.

The Arabic has also an allusion to this (pp. ٤, ٥, l. 21) وامر الجحيم.

The connexion of the Anaphora with the Peter-Gospel will be found worked out at length in von Schubert (*Peter-Gospel*, p. 182, with reference to Robinson, p. 26, n. 1). Besides the important coincidences we have mentioned, he notices some minor points.

1. Ev. Petri, c. 1. *Καὶ τότε κελεύει* 'Ηρώδης *ὁ* Βασιλεὺς *παρ[αλημ]φθῆναι τὸν* Κύριον.

Anaph. Pilati, r. A. p. 439. Τοῦτον *δὲ* 'Ηρώδης *καὶ* 'Αρχέλαος...*παρέδωκάν μοι*. r. B. p. 446. Τοῦτον *οὖν* 'Ηρώδης... *παραδεδώκασί μοι*.

Syriac, p. ܕ, ll. 3, 4. ܠܗ ܕܝܢ ܠܗܢܐ ܗܪܘܕܣ ܘܐܪܟܠܐܘܣ ...ܦܝܠ ܥܡ ܐܫܠܡܘܗܝ ܠܝ.

Arabic, pp. ٤, ٥, l. 4. فلهذا هيرودس وارشلاوس وقيلبس مع جميع الشعب اسلموه الي

2. Ev. Petri, c. 5. 'Ην *δὲ μεσημβρία, καὶ σκότος κατέσχε πᾶσαν τὴν* 'Ιουδαίαν.

Anaph. Pilati, r. A. p. 439. *τοῦ ἡλίου μέσης ἡμέρας σκοτισθέντος*. r. B. p. 446. *τοῦ ἡλίου κρυβέντος τελείως καὶ τοῦ πόλου σκοτεινοῦ φαινομένου ἡμέρας οὔσης*.

Syriac, p. ܗ, ll. 12, 13. ܘܟܕ ܐܙܕܩܦ ܗܘܐ ܗܘ ܚܫܘܟܐ ܢܦܠ ܥܠ ܡܫܟܐ ܐܝܟ ܗܘܐ ܚܫܘܟܐ ܙܐܪܒܐ ܥܠ ܟܠܗܘܢ ܒܪ̈ܝܬܐ.

Arabic, pp. ٤, ٥, ll. 7, 8. فلما صلب صارت ظلمة على الدنيا كلها واظلمت الشمس نصف النهار

3. Ev. Petri, c. 14. *ἀπήλθαμεν εἰς τὴν θάλασσαν.*

Anaph. Pilati (Tischendorf, r. A.). *εἴπατε τοῖς μαθηταῖς μου ὅτι προάγει ὑμᾶς εἰς τὴν* Γαλιλαίαν, *ἐκεῖ αὐτὸν ὄψεσθε*.

Syriac, p. ܘ, ll. 1, 2. ܕܗܐ ܠܓܠܝܠܐ ܦܩܕ ܠܗܘܢ: ܬܡܢ ܢܐܙܠܘܢ ܘܢܚܙܘܢܗܝ.

Arabic, pp. ٦, ٧, l. 2. قولوا للتلاميذ ان يتقدمونى الى الجليل

Von Schubert is led by his study of these documents to the conclusion that Pseudo-Peter, as well as Justin Martyr, was acquainted with some form of the Anaphora Pilati, and this would give a very early date to the kernel of these legends. It may be mentioned, as a vestige of them, that Pilate is canonized as a saint by the Abyssinian Church. See Stanley (*Eccl. Hist.* p. 13), and Neale (*Hist. of the Eastern Church*, p. 806).

I have been favoured by the Rev. Arthur Baker, R.N., with an account of a sheet of parchment, the sole remnant of an Ethiopic MS. unfortunately lost in the foundering of H.M.S. *Captain*, which contains a somewhat grotesque representation of Pilate in an attitude of prayer, and which describes first a controversy between Pilate and the Jews at the tomb of our Lord, and then (after a considerable hiatus in the MS.) the following words are put into Pilate's mouth (the translation being by Dr Montague R. James, of King's College): "I believe that Thou hast risen, and hast appeared to me, and Thou wilt not judge me, O my Lord, because I acted for Thee, fearing this from the Jews. And it is not that I deny Thy resurrection, O my Lord. I believe in Thy word, and in the mighty works which Thou didst work amongst them when Thou wast alive. Thou didst raise many dead. Therefore, O my God, be not angry with me because of what Thou didst...."

An account of this curious parchment was published by Mr Baker in the *Newbery House Magazine* for December, 1892.

The Anaphora, therefore, rests on a very complicated tradition, towards the determination of whose primitive form and subsequent history every version contributes.

The Syriac text published in this volume was copied by Mr J. Rendel Harris in 1893, from a late paper MS. (13th century?) in the library of St Katharine's Convent on Mount Sinai, No. 82 in Mrs Lewis's catalogue. The correspondence between Pilate and Herod, which follows it in the MS., has already been published by Wright (*Contributions to the Apocryphal Literature of the New Testament*, 1865) from a MS. in the British Museum (Add. 14,609).

The Arabic texts, which are probably translated from a Greek original approaching nearly to Tischendorf's recension A., possess a higher antiquity than the Greek texts published by him. The first one (A.) I took from a volume (No. 508 in my catalogue) consisting of 151 paper leaves, with 5 vellum leaves inserted, 20 centimètres by 15, which contained:

1. The Recognitions of Clement, as published in the present volume.

2. A sermon of St Dorotheus.

3. Histories of Holy Monks.

4. A story about the garments of our Lord.

5. Some ordinances of Mar Isaiah.

6. A sermon of Mar Isaac.

7. Another sermon.

8. The Anaphora and Paradosis Pilati.

9. Sermons by various Fathers, amongst others Anastasius Abbot of Sinai, and Thaumasius.

10. Another book attributed to Clement, akin to that known as the Book of Adam and Eve. (This I have copied.)

11. Songs of the Angels (also copied.)

12. Sermon of St John Chrysostom.

The last leaves of this book being lost, it was not possible to find the date. It was in 1893 that I made its acquaintance. When its text of the Anaphora was already in print, I visited Sinai for the third time with my sister in the early part of this year (1895) and I gladly seized the opportunity thus afforded to compare my transcripts with the MSS. I then found a charming little volume (No. 445) dated A.H. 183 (A.D. 799) which contained the Anaphora, as well as the text entitled "The Preaching of Peter," and which is thus four centuries earlier than any of the Greek texts hitherto known. The date A.D. 1233 which I had erroneously assigned to the book in making my rough catalogue two years previously, is

A. P.                                                                 *c* merely a date inscribed by an appreciative visitor. Lest there should be any doubt on the subject, I give a fac-simile of the page on which the date occurs*. I resolved not to give a mere collation of this the oldest text, but to print it side by side with the one from No. 508 already in type, marking the former as A. and the latter as B. Which is the earlier of the two recensions, seeing that the date of B. is lost, must be decided on palaeographical grounds alone. I cannot find anything similar to B. in the Palaeographical Society's publications. In Arabic as in Syriac a *yā* may be extended by a copyist so as to become a *lam*. This has evidently been the case with the name قيافاريس p. 2 A. where in B. p. 1 I at first read it قيافارلس. On the other hand, the word صالحين p. 9 A. is in B. p. 4 correctly صايحين.

Apocryphal as the story contained in the Anaphora Pilati is, we trust we have said enough to shew its undoubted claim to antiquity. We cannot but admire the author's truly Christian appreciation of the scope of Divine forgiveness, which could soften even Pilate's heart, and number him with the redeemed, like others perhaps more guilty still (Acts ii. 23–41). The Greek and Arabic recensions are free from any sentiment not fully authorized by Apostolic teaching.

## THE RECOGNITIONS OF CLEMENT.

THE Recognitions of the Roman Clement are too well known in their Latin as well as in their English dress to need any introduction to the scholar. They have been extant hitherto only in the Latin translation of Rufinus of Aquileia, who died A.D. 410†. It was first published by Sichardus (Basle, 1526) and since then by Cotelier (*Apostolic Fathers*, Paris, 1672), and by Gersdorf (Leipzig, 1838). A Syriac translation was also

---

\* See page ○○.

† Rufinus states in the preface to his work that he undertook it at the request of Sylvia (the pilgrim to Mount Sinai).

published by de Lagarde in 1861, from two MSS. in the British
Museum, the older of which was written at Edessa, A.D. 411.
The Greek original used by Rufinus was prefaced by a letter
from Clement to James the Lord's brother, bishop of Jerusalem,
which Rufinus left out, believing it to be of a later date.

The Arabic text given in this volume is contained in the MS.
No. 508 of the Sinai Catalogue, and is, compared to Rufinus's
Latin text, a very short narrative. It omits almost wholly the
discourses of Peter, and his discussions with Simon and others.
It would therefore be out of place here to do more than allude
to the question of the priority of the Recognitions or of
the Clementine Homilies to one another, a question which
has been debated with so much acumen by A. Schliemann,
Hilgenfeld, Uhlhorn, Ritschl, Lehmann, Lipsius and others.
Suffice it to say that through the labours of Uhlhorn, Hilgenfeld
and Ritschl, it is now pretty generally acknowledged that, as
Lehmann suggested, the three first books of the Recognitions
are the original document from which the Homilies were com-
posed, and that Books IV.–X. of the Recognitions were afterwards added from the Homilies (Lehmann, *Die Clementinischen
Schriften*, p. 21).

As to the date of the text and its origin, we have internal
evidence only to rely upon, though it is evident from the date
of the Syriac MS. Add. 12,150 in the British Museum that it
cannot be later than the fourth century. Hilgenfeld has pointed
out that Matthidia was the name of the sister of Trajan, mother-
in-law of Hadrian; and that the name Faustina was borne by
the wife of Antoninus Pius, as well as by her daughter, the
wife of Marcus Aurelius. The busts of these two ladies may be
seen in the British Museum. This suggests a date between
A.D. 150 and 170. The Recognitions, or a document closely
allied to them, are quoted by Origen, *Philocalia*, c. XXIII., *Com-
mentary on Genesis* 21, which was written A.D. 231.

καὶ Κλήμης δὲ ὁ Ῥωμαῖος Πέτρου τοῦ Ἀποστόλου μαθητὴς
συνῳδὰ τούτοις ἐν τῷ παρόντι προβλήματι πρὸς τὸν πατέρα ἐν
Λαοδικείᾳ εἰπὼν ἐν ταῖς περιόδοις, ἀναγκαιότατόν τι ἐπὶ τέλει τῶν

περὶ τούτου λόγων, φησίν, περὶ τῶν τῆς γενέσεως δοκούντων
ἐκβεβηκέναι, λόγῳ τεσσαρεσκαιδεκάτῳ, καὶ ὁ πατήρ.

Then follows a long quotation, evidently from the Greek
text translated by Rufinus, Book x. a. 10, 11, 12–23. It is
given in full by Robinson, *The Philocalia of Origen*, Cambridge,
1893.

All writers on the subject seem to agree that Syria is the
place of the origin of these documents, and that the author was
a Jewish Christian, who held doctrines distinctly Ebionistic.
This Arabic text does not go so deeply into questions of dogma
as the Latin or even the Syriac texts; yet even here we have
the superstitious reverence attached to water both in baptism
and ablutions; also the refusal of baptized Christians to eat
with unbaptized Christians; insomuch that Peter is represented
as continuing in the same narrow frame of mind for which his
brother-Apostle found it necessary to rebuke him (Galatians ii.
11–14). The Arabic text is, however, free from the outrageously
heathenish idea that Faustinian's face was changed by Simon
Magus to look like his own ; and the still more heathenish idea
that an Apostle could be guilty of a pious fraud by turning the
metamorphosis to account.

A. Schliemann has also pointed out that the hierarchical ideas
in the Recognitions point to a Jewish Ebionistic origin. Peter
appoints a bishop off-hand, and also presbyters and deacons,
the former of whom are of the mystical number twelve. It
deserves to be noted, however, that this Arabic text does not
take its actors to Rome, but seems to imply that they remained
in Syria; and it therefore does not attribute to Peter any breach
of the covenant made with Paul (Gal. ii. 9). Nor does it contain
any mention of James the bishop of Jerusalem, to whom the
Greek text used by Rufinus was addressed.

It is quite possible that this Arabic text is an epitome by
some Arab Christian monk who was more fascinated by the
interest of the narrative than anxious to edify his brethren by
translating the discourses. If so, we must grant that he has
shewn considerable literary skill, and has fully appreciated the

dramatic side of his documents. As to the story itself, there is nothing absolutely impossible in it. Communication between Rome and Athens was comparatively frequent in the days of the Empire; and if mere tent-makers like Priscilla and Aquila could have interests in several cities and countries, there is nothing unlikely in a noble Roman lady taking her children to Athens for their education and her own convenience. The only circumstance that in my humble judgment seems somewhat improbable, is that Faustinian should have been for several days in the island of Aradus, and have time to carry on a philosophical discussion with Peter's young followers: and yet that he and his wife should have needed Peter's intervention to recognize one another.

I have found another version of this Clement story in the British Museum XXVIII. (Add. 9965), bearing the comparatively late date of A.D. 1659, and followed by an account of Clement's martyrdom, by the same hand. The codex containing them is a paper 4to. of 235 leaves, the greater part being by the hand of Macarius, Patriarch of Antioch, the remainder by his disciple Paulus. I have thought it worth while to transcribe and translate them, because they shew the later development of the legend. I note the following variations between this MS. and the Sinai one:

1. In S. the name of Clement's father is Faustinus, in B.M. Fafestus; there is also a difference in the name of his eldest brother.

2. S. makes Clement meet and befriend Barnabas in Rome, whereas B.M. makes this happen at Alexandria.

3. In S. Clement is baptized before he meets his mother, in B.M. he is baptized along with her; S. makes Peter command Clement to fast for three days before his baptism, B.M. extends this period to three months, and makes Peter act very inconsistently in baptizing the people of Aradus without any such delay.

4. S. makes Matthidia give false names to her husband's

birth-place and her own, as well as to her sons; whereas B.M. makes her tell the true names at once. Perhaps the editor from whom Macarius translated felt that Peter's presence was a dangerous quarter in which to tell falsehoods.

5. In S. Niceta and Aquila reveal their identity at once when Peter has finished their mother's story, indeed, they have scarcely been able to restrain themselves throughout it; whereas in B.M. they are silent and lost in thought for hours afterwards. This is surely an artificial touch.

6. S. is quite free from the ungodly idea contained in B.M. and in the text of Rufinus, that an Apostle could be guilty of the stratagem of sending Clement's father to Antioch in the likeness of Simon.

7. S. does not take Peter and Clement to Rome at all; whereas B.M. makes the former formally instal the latter as his successor in its bishopric.

8. S. makes no mention of James the Lord's brother at all, whereas the narrative in B.M. is addressed to him.

I have placed marginal references to both the Recognitions and Homilies alongside the text of both S. and B.M. These must by no means be considered to imply perfect agreement, but only be used to facilitate comparison.

The Martyrdom of Clement, which follows the story of the Recognitions in the British Museum MS., can be interesting only to the student of folk-lore. The story of the Saint's providing water has a curious likeness to the modern experience of the veteran missionary Dr J. G. Paton, in the New Hebrides; the submarine temple suggests submerged ruins; and the miracle of the sea retreating would suggest an effect of the tides, had we the Atlantic to deal with instead of the Euxine.

The writing of this MS. is small and clear, final *hays* being very insignificant. A curious peculiarity is Macarius's incapability of spelling words from the roots حضر and ضَلَّ correctly; he invariably substitutes ظ for ض in both, though I have not convicted him of doing likewise in any other word. I have a

suspicion that he occasionally places the *ta* of the 8th form of the verb before its first root-letter instead of after it, as in
اتعلمنا p. ٣٩, l. 4; اتزوجت p. ٤٠, l. 15; اتجادل p. ٤١, l. 6; اتعرفا p. ٤٣, l. 20; واتقنوا p. ٤٣, l. 22; اتشفعى p. ٤٨, l. 23; اتناول p. ٥٠, l. 21; فاتناول p. ٥١, l. 2.

As it is possible, however, to treat the prefixed *Alif* as an interjection, and refer the verb to the 5th form, I have given Macarius the benefit of the doubt.

The only word for which I have been able to find no solution is القويص f. 197 b. l. 11.

## THE PREACHING OF PETER.

THIS story is from the same Codex No. 445, dated A.D. 799, from which I took recension A. of the *Anaphora Pilati*. It is a lively example of how mediæval monks managed to slake the universal human thirst for fiction. Probably such tales took a similar place within the cloistered fane to the modern religious novel in Puritan families; they were also quite as harmless and even more edifying.

The short biographies of James the son of Alphaeus and of Simon the son of Cleophas are from the Codex No. 539 in my catalogue. They are evidently almost purely legendary, and it does not seem to have occurred to their author that Alphaeus and Cleophas might possibly be the same person; had they been two individuals, Simon would have had a more certain relationship to the Lord than James. I was attracted to these tales from curiosity to see what might be the idea current amongst early Arab Christians in regard to the nature of that relationship, but they give no hint on a subject so profoundly interesting to us. I saw in the same volume a short biography of " James the Lord's brother," which I regret not having had time to copy, and I hope that any Arabic scholar who may go to Sinai will repair this omission.  Throughout the whole of these Arabic texts I have made no alteration from the MSS. except the change of final ا to ى, where the latter is now customary, and printing من اجل in full for the contracted form منجل.

Neglect of the subjunctive mood is so common to all these old Arabic writers that I fear we must give them a general absolution.  The few additional blunders I have thought proper to correct are indicated by the foot-notes.

In conclusion, I have to thank Dr Eberhard Nestle, of Ulm, for kindly revising my translation of Mr Harris's Syriac transcription; Mr J. F. Stenning, of Oxford, for taking some photographs of the *Anaphora Pilati* for me during his visit to Sinai in 1894; and my sister, Mrs S. S. Lewis, for reading over the Arabic proofs.

# ANAPHORA PILATI.

## TRANSLATION OF THE SYRIAC.

[1]The report of the notification concerning our Lord Jesus the Christ, which was sent by Pilate, governor of Palestine, to Tiberius Cæsar, the Emperor of Rome, in the city of Rome.

For in those days after the crucifixion of our Lord Jesus the Christ by command of Pontius Pilate, to whom was committed the dominion of Palestine and Phenicia, these things took place and happened in Jerusalem. Memoirs of [the things] that were done to our Lord Jesus the Christ by the hands of the Jews, by means of a writing of Pilate himself.[1] [2]He sent it to Tiberius Cæsarius to the city of Rome thus:

To the Worshipful, to the Ruler of the universe, Tiberius the victorious Emperor; Pontius Pilate, governor of the region of the East, of the cities of Phenicia. Being in great fear and in much trembling, I make known to thy majesty, O

---

[1] [*Arabic.*] om. The . . . himself.

[2] [*Arabic.*] B. In the name of the Father, and of the Son, and of the Holy Ghost, one God. A. This is the memorial of what was done to our Lord Jesus the Christ by command of Pilate the Pontius, ruler of the Jews, in the eighteenth year of the reign of Tiberius the Cæsar Emperor of Rome, in the nineteenth year from the beginning of the reign of Herod son of Herod king of the Jews, when the twenty-fifth day of Adar had passed; in the government of Rufus (B. and Rubilinus), and

Emperor, that at that time a short while ago, I make known, that in that city of priests, the most honoured of all cities, Jerusalem, all the people of the Jews delivered to me a certain righteous man who was called Jesus, bringing against him many accusations which were calumnious, but they were page 2 not able to convict him of anything, for they only shewed one heresy in truth against him; that Jesus had said to them that the Sabbath is nothing, neither the keeping of it. But he made many cures on this day of the Sabbath, by means of good works; for he opened the eyes of the blind and caused them to see; and the lame to walk, and he raised the dead. And he cured the paralysed, and gave them health, [those] who could not move their bodies, or stretch one of their muscles, and there was nothing at all that could be moved, except only the voice: and to these he gave strength that they should walk and run. And he commanded the sick, and they were healed. And the last thing that was greater than all, which is thought wonderful even for the gods: a dead man who had been four days in Sheol, he commanded by a word only, and he arose, he who was in the village of Bethany, and his body was stinking with foam and all his body was eaten by the earthworm.

---

in the fourth year of their rule, by command of Iusius son of Kia-farius, priests of the Jews, and all that happened after the cross and sufferings of the Lord, and the doings of the (B. two) chief priests and others of the Jews. And all that Nicodemus saw he wrote in the Hebrew tongue.

In these days Jesus was crucified by command of Pilate (B. the Pontius), in his dominion over Palestine and the coast, and this is the memorial which was made in Jerusalem by the Jews concerning the Christ, and which was sent up to Tiberius the Cæsar in Rome.

Him he raised, and commanded him to run, there being no appearance of a dead man about him at all, but like a bride-groom who goes out of the bride-chamber, thus he was perfect in all his appearance.

And to other people who were vexed by demons, and were chased from [their] dwelling, and had lived in the deserts and ate their [own] flesh, he caused all these to sit down in their houses like wise [people], and he drove the demons out of them, and drowned them in the sea by means of the swine.

And again the man whose hand was withered, and all his side, he cured by a word alone, and he arose quite whole without hurt.

And again the woman whose blood had run for eighteen years[1], when she touched his garment, was cured.

And also the damsel, the daughter of one of the chiefs of the Jews themselves, he raised from death as from a sleep. And again in the city of Nain, whilst they were going to bury a dead man, the son of a widow, and he saw that her grief was bitter and sore, he called him, and raised him, and made him turn with joy to his buriers.

But those chief priests accused him that he worked on the Sabbath day and cured all afflictions. But I think that this Jesus did also other miracles which were much greater

---

[1] [*Arabic.*] and her muscles and her joints were loosened by the flow of blood till she did not bear a human form, but resembled the dead who have no voice; and not one of the physicians who were in the towns could cure her, for there was no hope of life left in her; and [as] Jesus [was] passing, she received strength, and in the midst of the crowd laid hold of the hem of his garment, and from that hour she was strengthened and cured and went running to her town, Banias, from Capernaum. And that was not near it, a journey of six days.

And also another man born blind from his mother's womb, who had no eyes at all. He spat on the ground, and made clay and anointed the place of his eyes, and created eyes for him with which he might see, and sent him to the water of Siloam to wash.

(The stories of Jairus's daughter and of the widow's son are omitted.)

than these, that would be great and wonderful even from the gods whom we worship.

But this [man] Herod and Archelaus and Philip and Hannan and Caipha, those [men] delivered to me, with the multitude of the Jews. And they[1] raised a great sedition against me [2]on account of this [man] in a crowd that I should crucify him[2]. And I strove much to release him, and I could not. And when I saw page 3 the tumult that rose against me because of him, I gave sentence against him that he should be crucified, having scourged him beforehand with whips, not having found against this man one reason which condemned him to death among all the accusations that they brought against him. And when this Jesus was crucified on the wood, a great darkness took hold of all created things in the middle of the day; because the sun was darkened[3], and the light of the moon appeared like unto blood, [4]and many people of the Jews were swallowed up by the earth; and there were great thunderings and lightnings; and many graves were opened, and many dead people rose from their graves. And the twelve patriarchs with Abraham and Isaac and Jacob, those who had gone out of the world, about two thousand years ago[4], I saw them with my eyes in the body as they appeared also to all men. And they mourned and wept bitterly because of the great iniquity which took place, and because of the destruction of the Jews, and of their Law, for

---

[1] [*Arabic.*]   The people.

[2] *om.* on...him.

[3] at mid-day, and the stars did not shew their rays, and the moon was uncovered, and her light &c.

[4] and thus the veil of the temple of the Jews was torn, and with the force of the earthquake the rocks were rent, and in that terror

they could not even repose, on account of the earthquake that there was from six o'clock on Friday until the time that the Sabbath-day dawned. And at the time when the first day of the week dawned, there was a loud voice from Heaven, and a light shone seven times greater than [that of] every day. And at the time of the third hour of the night of the first day of the week there appeared a sun shining with its rays more than every day, and like lightning that flashes suddenly on a winter day, thus were seen men who were great and tall in stature, clothed in garments of glory and of wonder, who were very many and innumerable. And thus their voice went when they cried, as the voice of a great thunder, for they cried thus: [5]He who was crucified upon the wood of the cross, Jesus the Nazarene, who is God, has come again to life, and has risen from the grave.[5] [6]Arise, come, ye who were imprisoned in the lowest depths of Sheol.[6] Then the earth was cleft from above to the great abyss; nothing being seen of its foundations, [7]save only the waters of the abyss, those that are below the earth. And there was seen a crowd of people who had come to life and rose from among the dead. And thus they cried with those who cried from the height of heaven, The Saviour and the

---

the dead appeared and stood, as even the Jews testify that they saw Abraham and Isaac and Jacob the fathers, and Moses and Job who died, as these say, two thousand and five hundred years ago.

[5] [*Arabic.*] The God who was crucified is risen; he went up and gave his commands to Gehenna.

[6] O ye who were enslaved in the lower parts of the earth.

[7] and thus appeared the waters of the abyss, with the cry of those who were in Heaven, and the dead who rose and walked were very many; and he robbed Gehenna of its dead, and appeared to the women and said to them, Say to my disciples, that they go before me into Galilee, for there they shall see me.

Raiser of the dead said to his disciples, Behold he goeth before them into Galilee, there they shall go and see him[7]. And during all that night, the light never ceased to shine. And many of the Jews died and were swallowed up in the midst of the earth[1], [2]these who had stood up against Jesus. But I saw also a vision of dead [men], of those who had come to life and had risen, those whom I had never seen [before]. But these Jews, who remained and were concealed, went and saw[2]. I, however, was in great fear and trembling. I wrote the things that I saw which were done. And I sent these things to thy Majesty, O Emperor, having already put in these writings everything that was done by the Jews. And here I have sent it to the Majesty of thy Royalty. [3]O Lord, I salute thee.[3]

page 4

## PARADOSIS PILATI.

And when these letters were written and sent up to Rome the city of the empire, and Tiberius Cæsar knew them; and they were brought up and read before him; all they who were gathered before him there were seized with a great wonder[4] about this, because of the great iniquity and wickedness that had been

---

[1] [*Arabic.*] so that many were not found in the morning of those who did as they did to Jesus. And all the synagogues of the Jews who were in Jerusalem fled, and not one appeared.

[2] om. these...saw.

[3] *om.* O...thee.

[4] when they heard that through the sin of Pilate the earthquake and the darkness had come upon the whole world. om. about...Pilate.

done by Pilate. Then Tiberius Cæsar was filled with a great anger, and ⁵his rage mounted up against Pilate like smoke from a furnace. And in the rage of his anger⁵ he sent Romans⁶ to bring him from Jerusalem to Rome in great disgrace, like a man who is a malefactor. Then the Romans came down according to the commandment of Cæsar; and they took Pilate and bound him with fetters of iron, and thus they took him up to Rome beside Cæsar. Then the Emperor Tiberius having heard that Pilate had come up to Rome, ⁷commanded that a tribune should be prepared for him, in one of the temples of the heathen gods. When all his own council were assembled with him, and all those who held positions of power, and all the forces of his dominion were gathered, he went up and⁷ sat in the temple on the tribune. Then he commanded that they should make Pilate stand before the judgment-seat. And when Pilate went up and stood before him, Tiberius answered and said to him, What are these things that thou hast done in thy wickedness? Wonderful things like these had been told to thee, and thou hast dared wickedly to crucify that man, and thou hast clothed the whole world with darkness by thine iniquity. Then Pilate answered and said to him, O Emperor, I am blameless in this. They who are guilty of this crime are the multitude⁸ of the Jews. And Cæsarius answered

---

⁵ *om.* his...anger.

⁶ i.e. Roman soldiers.

⁷ *om.* commanded...and.

⁸ religion.

and said to him, And who are these? Pilate said to him,
Herod who is called Archelaus, and Philip, and Hannan, and
Caiapha, and all the multitude of the Jews. The Emperor
then returned him an answer and said, By what impulse didst
thou adhere to them and consent to them and obey their
counsel? Pilate answered and said to him, All their nation
page 5 are seditious and disobedient people, and, my Lord, they do
not obey the great authority of thy power. Then Cæsar
answered and said to him, And when they had delivered him
to thee, it was thy duty to imprison him, and take watch over
him, and to send him to me with great circumspection by
means of the soldiers of my kingdom, and not be persuaded
by the advice of the Jews and crucify him, a man who was righteous, and who had done these good works, when thou hadst
confessed and said by means of the certified[1] report [2]which
was sent by thee to us when he went to be crucified, that[2] this
is the Christ the King of the Jews. And when he said these
things, and mentioned the name of the Christ, all the gods that
were in that temple fell down and were broken, and thus they
were ground [in pieces] like powder[3]. Then all the crowd who
stood there before Cæsar were in great fear and trembling
[4]because of the fall of the gods, and because of the style of the

---

[1] *Syriac*, certifying.

[2] [*Arabic.*] that when thou didst wish to crucify him thou didst
write on a tablet.

[3] [*Arabic.*] *add* in that place where Cæsar sat with all his officers.

[4] *om.* because...spoken.

words that were spoken⁴. Trembling took hold of them. Thus each of them, one by one, went up to his house, wondering in his mind at what had happened.

Now Tiberius Cæsar had commanded that Pilate should be imprisoned and carefully guarded, ⁵when this was known in truth about the Son⁵. ⁶And the next day he had a judgment-seat in the Capitol of the Empire.⁶ And he went up and sat there with all his Senate. And he commanded that Pilate should come before him. And when Pilate came up and stood before the judgment-seat, Cæsar began again to ask Pilate, and thus he spake to him, Tell me truly, O wicked villain, for on account of the iniquity and wicked-ness which thou hast done, ⁷and hast stretched forth [thy] hand upon the Son,⁷ even now thy wicked and daring works are seen, O villain! Thus it happened to all the gods, and they fell ⁸from their places and were broken and ground like powder, and perished from the earth⁸. Tell me truly, who was that man that was crucified? for lo! his name alone has destroyed all those gods. And Pilate answered and said to him, ⁹His own memorials in truth certify that he is the Son of God.⁹ Even I have been convinced by his works that he is very much

---

⁵ [*Arabic.*] till he should know the affair of Jesus by examination.

⁶ *om.* And...Empire.

⁷ *om.* and...Son.

⁸ *om.* from...earth.

⁹ The report which I sent to thee about it is true.

A. P.                                                                              2

greater than those gods whom we worship. And Cæsar answered and said to him, And why therefore didst thou do to him such deeds as thou didst write to me, [1]when thou didst not know that any wicked thing had been done by him against our kingdom[1]? And Pilate answered and said to him, On account of the impiety and quarrelsomeness which they raised unjustly against me, they who are Jews, I did this to him. page 6 Then Tiberius Cæsar was filled with a great anger, [2]and his wrath rose like the smoke from a furnace[2]. And he took counsel quickly with all his officers. Then he commanded that an edict should be written against the Jews thus, To Lucianus chief and commander of the district of the East, governor of the whole province, greeting. [3]Because a certain unlawful thing was done to-day, in the daring deed that was done by certain inhabitants of Jerusalem and of the towns that are round about it, who are Jews, transgressors of the law, [4]they who did a wicked and atrocious deed to a certain god who was called the Son, by means of Pilate, by the compulsion that they raised against him, and they assembled and rose in insurrection and in great contention and crucified him[4], and as if owing to these wicked deeds which they did, all created things nearly perished by the darkness that was over all the earth. [5]For the earth shook and the graves were opened, and the rocks were rent, and the sun did not appear, and the whole world

---

[1] [*Arabic.*] when thou wast not ignorant of it, if thou didst not wish evil against my kingdom.

[2] *om.* and...furnace.

[3] *add* I fear.

[4] that they condemned and crucified a god who was called Jesus.

[5] *om.* For...destruction.

was nearly left to destruction.[5] But [6]thou, immediately on receiving this commandment which is sent to thee from us[6], seek and gather to thee all the Roman troops, and take them and go to Jerusalem, and make there a great captivity, as by our own command, having scattered and dispersed them amongst all nations for bondservice, [7]all those who are of the nation of the Jews. Remove and scatter their tribe, having taught fear to all the tribes that they do not venture nor do a deed like this in the ire and anger of their rage[7].

When this command went down and arrived in the eastern province, [8]and was given into the hands of Lucianus governor of all the region of the East, he was in great fear by reason of this command. But he left the Jews in their former religion as they were. And those Jews who were left in foreign lands he subjugated them to the nations. And this holds good and has continued to this day[8]. And when these things were done by Lucianus, and were made known to the Emperor Tiberius, they were pleasing to him. Again, Tiberius commanded with respect to Pilate that he should come before him, and he put questions concerning him[9], and he commanded one of the executioners to take off Pilate's head[10]. Then that blessed

---

[6] *om.* thou . . . us.

[7] and banish them from Jerusalem.

[8] Lucianus both heard and obeyed the command of Cæsar to the letter; and he made captive all the nation of the Jews, and those who remained among the nations, he commanded that they should be subjugated unto this day.

[9] Jesus.

[10] *add.* because he had stretched it out against Jesus the God.

one, when he went and arrived ¹at the place where he was about to be crowned by his Lord, entreated the executioner, saying, I entreat thee, my brother, for the love of our Lord Jesus the Christ, that thou have patience with me a little that I may pray and supplicate to him on account of whom I bear this sentence of death by means of this sharp sword. And when Pilate had said these things, he turned towards the east, page 7 and knelt before his Lord¹, and began to entreat his Lord Jesus the Christ, I beg of Thee, Almighty God, our Lord Jesus the Christ, who came for our salvation ; receive, Lord, the prayer of Thy servant at this time, and absolve, Lord, and forgive me all [in which] I have failed and sinned before Thee. I knew not what I did. And, Lord, reckon not it as sin to me, nor destroy¹ me with the mad people of the Jews, because I did not wish to soil my hands with Thy holy blood. ²And just because of this very thing I took water and washed my hands, and I said that I am pure from the blood of that just man.²  And when I had done this, then the cursed people of the Jews rose against me in insurrection. ³And Thou, Lord, knowest that from fear of Cæsar I delivered Thee into their hands.³  And Thou, my Lord and my God, knewest that I did this not knowing what I did. Lord, do not count this sin to me and destroy me, ⁴but remember

---

[Arabic.]   ¹ at the place of execution, he prayed silently and said,
Lord, do not destroy, etc.

² om. And . . . man.

³ om. And . . . hands.

⁴ and be not angry with me nor with.

me and[4] Thy servant Procla, her who stands with me in the conflict at this time, and in this bitter hour of death, [5]her who saw in prophecy when Thou camest to be crucified; remember not this sin to me, Lord, nor require it at my hands[5], but absolve and forgive us our debts and our sins, and make us stand on the side of the righteous, and may we be counted with them in Thy kingdom. And when Pilate had finished his prayer, behold, a voice came to him from Heaven, saying, Men upon earth shall call thee blessed, and all the tribes of the people, because that in thy days and by thy hands was completed and perfected all that is written in the prophets concerning me. And thou therefore shalt be a witness to me in that second coming of mine, when I shall come to judge the twelve tribes of Israel, and them who do not confess me and believe in my holy name. [6]And when this voice came to him and spake with him, he gave thanks, and knelt on the earth, and said to the executioner, Come near now and finish what thou art commanded by Cæsar.[6] And when the executioner came near and struck with the sword, and took off Pilate's head, then an angel of God came down from Heaven, and he received Pilate's head. [7]Now Procla his wife was standing and looking at him.[7] And when she[8] saw the angel of God who received the head of her husband, then she was filled with great joy; and in the joy of her heart she

---

[*Arabic.*]  [5] her whom Thou didst teach to prophesy when it was Thy will to be crucified, and do not condemn me and her for my sin.

[6] *om.* And . . . Cæsar.

[7] *om.* Now . . . him.

[8] Procla his wife.

gave up her soul to her Lord, and she was buried with her husband. [1]And they finished their conflict with a good testimony. And they were thought worthy of the Paradise of God. And they mediate on behalf of sinners that they may repent and live. May their prayers be a wall to us![1] [2]Amen, and Amen.

---

[*Arabic.*] [1] *om.* And . . . us.

[2] And to our Lord Jesus the Christ be praise and glory and power from henceforth and to everlasting. Amen.

# RECOGNITIONS OF CLEMENT.

*(From a MS. in the Convent at Mount Sinai.  No. 508.)*

IN the name of the Father, and of the Son, and of the Holy Ghost, one God.  The Christ is God, my strength, my help, and my hope.  This is the tale of [how] Clement recognized his parents and his brothers by means of Peter the Apostle, chief of the Apostles, blessed in the faith ; and this is the teaching of the above-mentioned Saint Peter, while he was at Tripolis.

"It is necessary that love to God should be greater than that to parents and children, for He is the cause of all ; and it is difficult for us to know what God is, but we are sure that He is God.  And do not think that ye are believers, when ye are without baptism, because by it the figure of grace is found in the water, recognizing those who are baptized in the name of the Blessed Trinity, who saves from future punishment ; and therefore hasten to the water, for it alone is able to quench that fire.  And when he said that, he dismissed the crowd."  And when I Clement had completed three months with him, he commanded me to fast for three days, and then we went to fountains of water on the sea-shore, and he baptized me there and with me Maroones, the man who had entertained us.  Then page 2 he appointed him bishop of Tripolis, and twelve presbyters, with deacons.  Then he left the people of Tripolis, and went out to Antioch in Syria.

And the cause of my meeting him was this.  While I was in the city of Rome, in my youthful years, I had carried chastity and righteousness to a great length, as also the recollection of death, and meditation about the soul, whether it is

mortal or immortal, and about this world, whether it had a beginning or not, and whether it will perish or not.   And whilst I
thought on these things, I did not cease frequenting the place of
philosophers and wise men, and I did not find anything more
from the Porch than a deceitful and vain thing, and I thought
I would go to Egypt to those magicians [who foretell] about
the dead, and while I thought about this, lo! news was spread
about in the empire of Tiberius concerning a man in the land
of Judæa who was preaching the eternal kingdom of God and
who confirmed that by many mighty deeds.   And when this
was so, behold, Barnabas came to Rome preaching the Christ,
page 3 and the wise men were mocking him.   And meanwhile I knew
in him a righteous purpose ; and I adopted his evidence, and I
forsook like dogs those who do not accept the word of salvation ;
and I took Barnabas, and I entertained him at my house, and
I heard speech from him ; and when they were going out to
the land of Judæa, I went out with him, and in fifteen days
we came to Cæsarea ; and I heard that Peter was in it,
and that he intended [to have] a contest with Simon the
next day ; and when I went to his dwelling, Barnabas
brought me in to him.   And Peter received me with much affection, and he was very glad of what I had done to benefit
Barnabas in Rome, and he confirmed my vocation, and commanded me to come to him, as he intended to travel to
Rome ; and when I promised him this, I asked him about the
soul and about the world, and he made clear to me briefly by
examination the folly that enters into people by means of sin,
and that is what overclouds the minds of people like smoke.
page 4 And he explained to me the coming of the Christ, and the
resurrection to life.   And in the morning, behold, Zacchæus
came saying that Simon had postponed the contest for seven
days.   Peter completed his teaching of us about the science of
the world, according to what the Holy Spirit gave him.   And
after this we went to Tripolis, to the place in which I was baptized, and from thence Peter sent Niceta and Aquila with others to
Laodicea, and told  them to wait for him at the door of the city.

But I and he went to Antaradus, and I thanked him for taking me with him as his follower, and he said to me, 'If I send thee to a place to buy for us what is necessary, wilt thou die?' And I answered and said to him, 'Thou art to me instead of my father and my mother, and my brothers; thou hast been the cause of my knowing the truth; and thou hast made me equal to great people. Wilt thou therefore put me in the place of service?' And Peter answered joking and said to me, 'Dost thou think that thou hast never been a servant? And who <sub></sub> page 5 will watch over my undressing and dressing? and who will prepare for me the many dishes that are necessary to the cooks, and this in the greatness of skill which is designed for luxurious people for the gratification of desire which is a great satisfaction, and I am clothed by it with abundance; and do not imagine that thou shalt know anything of this if thou art with me, for I do not get anything but the smallest bit of bread, and some oil with a little pulse; and all my wardrobe is these rags which thou lookest upon, and I need nothing else, for my mind looks on the good things that are eternal, and does not turn to what is contemptible. And I am surprised at thee, for thou art a man brought up in the enjoyment of the world, and thou hast despised all this, and thou art contented with things in <sub></sub> page 6 moderation. But I and my brother Andrew were brought up in orphanage and poverty and misery, and we were accustomed to toil and that we should bear fatigue. For this reason I will endure from thee toil and service to thyself.' And when I heard this from him I shuddered at it, and took an example on hearing this from a man whom the world cannot equal, and my eye wept. And when he saw me crying, he said to me, 'Why are thine eyes weeping?' And I answered him, saying, 'In what have I sinned against thee, that thou causest me to hear this speech?'

And Peter said, 'If I did wrong in saying I would serve thee, thou didst a greater wrong at the first when thou didst not see that, and there is no equality in this, yet it is fitting that I should <sub></sub> page 7 do this to thee.'

'But thou, O Apostle from God, Saviour of our souls, it is

A. P.  3

not fitting that thou shouldst do this.'   And Peter answered and
said, 'Behold, I would have accepted thy opinion, if it were not
that our Lord, who came for the salvation of the world, to whom
alone be honour, bore service, that He might persuade us not to
be ashamed to serve our brethren.   And He washed my feet and
hands, saying, Thus do to thy brethren.'   And I Clement
said to him, 'I thought I should conquer thee in speech, and I
was a fool, but I thank God who has put thee in the place
page 8 of parents.'   And Peter said to me 'Hast thou any kinsfolk?'
And I said to him, 'There are noble men in my family nearly
related to Cæsar the Emperor.   And he, the husband of my
mother, possesses dignity, and by her we are three boys, twins
before me, as my father told me, and I do not even know them,
nor my mother, except by a faint recollection; and after them
my mother gave birth to me, and her name was Matthidia, and
my father's name was Faustinian and my brothers', Faustus and
Faustinianus.   And when I was in my fifth year, my mother
saw a vision in her sleep, as my father related to me afterwards,
that if the woman did not take her children immediately and go
out of Rome and travel for ten years, she would perish, both
page 9 she and they.   But my father, when he heard this, carried them
into a ship, with provisions, secretly, with many servants, and
sent them to travel to Athens, and he kept me only with him in
order to console me, being overwhelmed with grief thereat.
And when a year had passed after that, my father sent to
Athens goods and money, in order that he might know their
state; and the messengers went, and did not return.   And in the
third year he sent others for that [purpose], and they departed, and
came in the fourth year to tell that they had not found the lads,
nor their mother, and that these had never got to Athens at all;
and they did not find a trace of them.   And when my father
page 10 heard this, he sorrowed with a great sorrow, and he was in much
perplexity, but he neither knew how to find [them] nor where to
weep for them.   And he went to the shore of the sea, and I with
him, and he began to ask the sailors from every place where ships
had been wrecked for four years past, if any of them had seen a

drowned woman with her boys; and he did not fall in with the certainty of the matter, for no one can explore the expanse of the ocean. Thereupon he made me his heir in Rome, and appointed guardians over me; and I that day was twelve years old, and he went from Rome in a ship, and departed to places to look for them. And now I have not heard news of him, nor [seen] writing, and I do not know if he is alive or dead, whilst I think that he must have died, and now to-day it is twenty years since page 11 he separated from me.' And when Peter heard this, his eyes wept from pity, and he said to those believers that were with him, 'One gains experience by what this man's father hath suffered. It shews concerning believers who are not vain heathen, who suffer here without reward in the last day, that those of the believers who are tried here endure suffering for the forsaking of their sins by means of it.' And when Peter said this, one of those present answered before all, and besought Peter, saying, 'Behold, to-morrow our journey will be to the island of Aradus in the sea that thou mayest see it. And there are there great pillars of vine-wood, and the sight of them is wonderful.' And Peter allowed us to go, and said to us, 'When page 12 ye arrive, do not go all of you together to the wonderful place, that no misfortune befall you.' And we went, and came to the island, and we got down out of the ship where the pillars were, and every one of us began to turn to some of the marvels that were there. But whilst Peter went to the pillars, behold, a woman sitting outside the gates asking alms. And when Peter saw her, he said to her, 'O woman, what is defective in thy limbs, that thou hast submitted to this humiliation of begging, and thou dost not increase what God has given thee by the work of thy hands, so that thou couldst even give bread to me from day to day?' And the woman sighed, and said, 'O would that I had hands able for service and work, but they are in the form page 13 of hands, yet they are dead, even when I bite them with my teeth.' And Peter answered and said, 'And what is the cause that obliges thee to do this?' And the woman said, 'The cause of it is only weakness; if I had boldness or strength, I would have thrown away my life from a mountain, or in the deep, and I would have had rest from the sorrows and the cares with which my people reproach me.' Said Peter, 'And are those who kill themselves saved from punishment, or do they suffer more of it in Gehenna with the souls who did thus to kill them?' And the woman said, 'O would I were sure that in Gehenna there are living souls, that I might go there and see my loved ones, even page 14 if I were in torment.' And Peter said, 'And what is it that grieves thee, O woman, tell me ; and if I knew perhaps I could cure thee, and convince thee that in Gehenna there are living souls, and give thee skill that thou shouldst not long (to go) with them to drowning, or to anything else, and that thou mayest go out of the body without torment.' And she was glad at the promise, and she began to relate to him, saying, " I am a woman who was possessed of dignity, and a nobleman wedded me, a man of position, related to Cæsar the Emperor. And I had twin sons by him, and I had another son besides them, and after that the brother of my husband fell in love with me, and I persuaded him to live in chastity, and I did not tell my husband of his wicked desire¹ towards me. And I resolved that I would not consent to him, nor defile the couch of my husband, besides exciting enmity between them, and that would be a reproach to page 15 me before all my people, and I resolved on going out of the city with my son for a short time till this bad wind should cease and vengeance should pass from me, and I left my other son with his father that he might be comforted by him, and I dreamt in a dream as if I saw a vision in the night saying to me, 'O woman, go out with thy children from here until a time that I will shew thee thy return, and if not, thou shalt perish with thy husband and children.' And therefore I did [it], and when I told this to my husband he shuddered at that, then he rose, and carried me into a ship with my boys, and many servants, and much goods, and sent us to Athens, and while we travelled on the sea, the winds arose against us, and the waves came over us, and we were engulphed in the night, and every one who was

¹ lit. desire of wickedness.

with us was drowned and I, miserable being, was thrown with a page 16
wave to the side of a rock, and I was inveigled by it (into) a hope
of finding my boys alive. On that account, I did not throw myself
to the depths and go to rest, and this, by my life, would have been
easy then, when I was overwhelmed with grief. And when the
dawn approached I began to turn and grope for my drowned sons,
and I mourn and bewail them with tears, whilst I did not see one
of them nor their drowned bodies; and when the people of the
place saw me, they pitied me and covered me. Then they
sought for my boys in the depths, and did not find them. And
there came to me women comforting me, and they were reminded
of the misfortunes and the griefs they had suffered like to what
had befallen me, and that was a thing that increases my grief
because there were no other misfortunes but [such as] mine with
which they consoled me. And they invited me to go to them
(two) and I went to a poor woman when she invited me to go to page 17
her, and she said to me, 'I had a husband, who died by drowning
in the sea, and left me that day, being of my own age, and since
then I have known no man, though many invited me to wedlock,
and I preferred chastity and piety towards my husband. Come,
we will go into one life and one household,' and I lived with her
that she might keep her affection for her husband. And after
that I had a pain in my hand, and the woman my house-
companion had a paralytic stroke there in the house, and since
then for some time I sit here begging alms for myself and for
my friend. And now I have explained to thee my affair and
my story, and fulfil now thy promise to me, that thou mayest
give me the cure, by means of which it will be possible for me
to hasten from this world with my friend." And when the
woman said this, Peter fell the more into thought, and he was
then standing, and I Clement came up to Peter, and said to page 18
him, 'O good Teacher, where hast thou been, for I have been
seeking thee for some time. What dost thou command us to
do?' And he said, 'Go forward and wait for me in the ship.'
And I did as he commanded me. And he renewed the ques-
tioning of the woman, and said to her, 'Tell me about thy

family, and thy city, and thy children, and their names, and I
will give thee the medicine.' And the woman did not wish to
tell him about that, and she began to tell him untruthfully, that
she might get the medicine. And she said to him, 'I am a
woman of Ephesus, and my husband was from Sicily,' and she
changed the names of her boys; and Peter saw that she was
trustworthy, and said to her, 'I had been thinking, that thou
wouldst have had a good fortune of joy this day, because I thought
that thou wert a woman whose affairs I know.' And the woman
adjured him, saying, 'I ask you to tell me what thou knowest, for
I do not think that among women there is one more wretched than
I.' And Peter began to relate to her truly, and said, 'There is
with me a lad my follower, in search of the certain knowledge of
page 19 God, and he is from Rome; besides, he told me about a father
whom he had, and twin brothers, and he believed that his
mother, as his father had told him, saw in a vision that she
should go out of Rome with her sons that she might not perish
with her husband, and she went out, and he does not know what
became of her, and that his father went in search of her, and
news of him failed also, and he does not know what became of
him.' And when Peter said this, the woman fell in a faint, and
Peter came forward, and took her hand, and said to her, 'Have
confidence, and trust me, and tell me truly what thou hast
to do with that.' As she recovered from the faint, and wiped
her face, she said, 'Where is this lad whom thou didst
tell me of?' And Peter said, 'Tell thou me first thy affair,
and I will shew thee him.' And she said, 'I am the mother
of this boy.' Said Peter, 'What is his name?' She said,
page 20 'Clement is his name.' And Peter said, 'He is the youth who
is present, and I commanded him to wait for me in the ship.'
And she fell down and did homage to him. And she said,
'Hasten first to the ship, that thou mayest show me my only
son, for when I see him, I have seen my boys who were drowned
here.' And Peter said to her, 'I will do this to thee, but when
thou seest him, be silent until thou comest down from the island.'
And the woman said, 'I will do so.' And Peter took her by

the hand, and brought her near to the ship. And when I saw
him holding a woman by the hand, I smiled, then I honoured
him for that, and I began to lead the woman, and when I caught
her hand, she cried with a loud voice, weeping and embracing
me, and she began to kiss me. And I, because I did not know
the thing, thought she was insane, or bewitched, and I pushed
her from me. And Peter said, 'Why, my son, dost thou push
thy mother from thee?' And when I heard this from him, that
she was my mother, my heart was troubled, and my eyes wept,
and I threw myself towards her and my heart warmed to her, page 21
and weeping overcame me for joy and pity, and I kissed her; and
all the people who were there came near us, hurrying to see the
beggar woman, how she had recognised her son. And when we
wished to go out from the island, my mother said to me, 'O my
beloved son, it is my duty to say good-bye to the woman who
received me, and besides, she is a paralysed woman, bed-ridden
in the house.' And when Peter heard [this], he marvelled at the
sense of the woman, and he commanded that the paralysed
woman should be carried on a couch, and they brought her to him.
And when they came near, Peter said, the people listening, 'If
I am an apostle of Christ, let these people now believe, that God
is the only one, Creator of all, and the restoration of this woman
is complete.' And when Peter said this, the woman rose whole,
and did obeisance to Peter, and asked him about these things. page 22
And he convinced her, and she knew the certainty of the thing;
and when all the people heard they wondered with a great
wonder, and Peter made them a speech about religion and
about the last day. He said, 'Whosoever wishes to hear
the certainty about God for the salvation of his soul, let
him travel to Antioch, as I have resolved to stay there for
three months; and more obligatory than absence for the merchandise of the gains of the world [is] the search for the salvation of souls, and the gain of the other [world].' And after
the speech of Peter to the people, I gave a thousand drachmas
to the woman whom Peter had cured, and entrusted them to
an honest man, and recompensed the women who all had known
my mother; and we travelled to Antaradus with Peter, and my

mother and the rest; and when we arrived at the house, my mother asked me, saying, 'How is thy father, O my son?' and I said to her, 'From the time when he went out in search of page 23 thee no trace was known of him'; and when she heard that she sighed and grieved. And after a day we went out to Laodicea, and when we came near to it, behold, before the gates disciples of Peter, Niceta and Aquila, and they met us and took us to the house; and when Peter saw the place suitable, he was pleased to stay there ten days, and Niceta and Aquila asked me, saying, 'Who is this woman?' and I said to them, 'This is my mother, whom God permitted me to know by the forethought of my lord Peter'; and when I said this, Peter explained to them the certainty of the thing, how it was, according as I had related it about my mother, according as he heard from her, and he it was who had led us to a knowledge of each other. And when Peter said this, they marvelled much when they heard Peter page 24 about the woman and her recollection of her sons Faustus and Faustinianus, and they were astonished at the tale. And they said, 'Do we see? is this a vision or the truth? if we are not be-witched it is true.' And they beat upon their faces, and they said, 'We are Faustus and Faustinianus, and our hearts were straitened when thou didst begin the tale, and we held firm till we should hear the end of the tale, because many of the things are like one another. And this by my life is our mother, and this is our brother.' And when they said this, they em-braced me with much weeping, and they kissed me, and they went in to our mother, and found her asleep. And Peter said to them, 'Do not wake her, lest an emotion of joy overcome her suddenly, and her soul grow small within her.' And when our mother awoke, Peter began to say to her, 'I will instruct thee, O woman, about our religion, and our faith in God; we page 25 believe in one God, Creator of all this visible world, and we keep His commands, and sanctify and honour [our] parents; and we live a pure life, and have no communion with the heathen in meat or in drink, unless they are baptized in the name of the Father, and of the Son and of the Holy Ghost. And if there is a father or mother or wife or son or brother unbaptized, we do not trust him, and do not be grieved if thy son is bound by this unless thou becomest like him.' And when she heard this, she said, 'And what is necessary, that I should not be baptized to-day, and that I should not come to this, because my soul has hated false gods, because they inspire the reverse of chastity, on account of which I fled from Rome with my sons Faustus and Faustinian?' And when our mother said this, my brothers Niceta and Aquila did not wait, but they [were] overjoyed and they embraced her and kissed her. And the woman said, page 26 'What is this thing?' Said Peter, 'O woman, keep thy presence of mind. These are thy sons Faustus and Faustinianus, whom thou didst think were drowned in the sea, how are they here before thee?' 'The sea swallowed them in the middle of the night, and how is the one called Niceta, and the other Aquila?' 'Let them tell us now that we and thou may know.' And when Peter said this, the woman fell in a faint from joy, and we restored her with great labour, and when she sat up, she said to us, 'I beg of you, my beloved sons, tell me what happened to you in that night.' And my brother Niceta said, 'I relate to thee, O my mother, that in that night when our ship was wrecked they carried us into the boat, to make merchandise of page 27 us, and they rowed with us to the land, and came with us to Cæsarea, and they tormented us there with hunger, and beating, in order that we should not say anything that did not suit them. And they changed our names, and sold us to a Jewess, whose name was Justa, and she bought us and educated us, and when we came to years of discretion, we acquired a sure faith in God, and we began disputing and conversing that the godlessness of all the heathen might be reproved; and we learnt the sayings of philosophy, that by this we might examine vain philosophies and reasonings. And we associated with a man, a wizard, whose name was Simon, and we had much affection for him, and he nearly led us astray. And it came to us that there was a prophet in the land of Judæa, and everyone who believed in him would live without sorrow or death, and we thought it was Simon; and after that we met a disciple of our master Peter, whose name was Zacchæus, and he exhorted us much and page 28 hurried us from the wizard, and conducted us to Peter, and he led us to the knowledge of the truth. And we seek from God that he would count thee worthy to welcome thee to the grace to which we have come, that we may be filled with grace towards one another. This is the reason why thou didst think that we were drowned that night, and we also thought that thou hadst perished in the sea.' And when Niceta said this, our mother ran to Peter and said, 'I ask and beg of thee that thou wouldst baptize me, that I may not be deprived one day of intercourse with my children.' And we begged this of him; and he commanded her to fast for three days, then after that he baptized her in the sea, in presence of her children, and we took food with her, and we rejoiced at this in the glory of God and page 29 the teaching of Peter, and in the knowledge we had got of our mother; and we learnt that chastity is the cause of salvation to the nations; and after that day Peter took us to the harbour, and we washed there, and prayed. And behold, an old man sitting there looking towards us, and observing our prayer closely, and after we had prayed, he approached us to reprove us and to say that everything happens by fortune, and that invocation and prayer are useless; and we remained three days to persuade him to change his opinion of this thing. And thereupon, during our discourse to him, we were calling him 'O Father'; and he was calling us, 'O my sons.' And this was a providence from God, because by it we began to know this word; and Aquila said to me and to Niceta, 'Why do you call this stranger 'Father'?' And my brother said to me, 'Do not complain of this,' and we continued in our talk to him, and he in that opinion of his, and he said 'Although the discourse has convinced me, yet I think of my wife, whose star and whose page 30 fortune was in vice, and she fled from wickedness on account of the disgrace, and she was drowned in the sea.' And I Clement said to him, 'And how dost thou know that the woman when she fled did not marry one of the slaves, and that she died?' 'I know certainly, that she did not marry, because she was chaste, and after her death, my brother related to me how she loved him at first and he in fidelity towards me and his continence

in his chastity, did not wish to defile my bed. And she, poor
creature, in her fear of me and of disgrace, used an artifice,
and she is not to be blamed, for this was fated against
her, and she feigned that she had seen a vision and she
said to me that 'if I remain here, I shall perish with
my sons.' And when I heard that from her, verily, through
my desire for her safety and [that of] her sons, I sent
her, and I kept with me a third son whom I had, as she
asserted that she saw in her dreams.' And when I heard page 31
this from him, I said, ' Perhaps this is my father,' and my eye
wept. And when my brothers sprung forward, wishing to em-
brace him, Peter prevented them, and said to them, ' Be silent
till it pleases me.' And Peter answered and said to the old
man, ' What is the name of thy son, the youngest boy ? ' And
the old man said, ' His name is Clement.' And Peter answered
him and said, ' If I shew thee to-day thy chaste wife with her
three sons, wilt thou believe that a chaste mind is able to
conquer animal emotions, and that my discourse which I made
to thee about God is the truth ?' And the old man said, ' Just
as what thou hast promised me cannot be, so there cannot be
(anything) without fate.' Said Peter, ' I call those present to
witness that this day I present to thee thy wife with her three
sons alive in her chastity. And the proof of this is my knowing the certainty of the thing better than thee. And I tell page 32
thee all that she related, in order that thou mayest know and
all these may know all this.' And when Peter said this, he began
to relate, saying, ' This man whom ye see, my brethren, in his
ragged raiment, he is of the people of Rome, of a great lineage,
and noble dignity, akin to Cæsar, and his name is Faustinianus ;
and he married a noble woman, and her name is Matthidia ; and
he had three sons by her, two of them twins, and the third younger
than they, whose name is Clement, and this is he, and these
are the others, the one Aquila, and the other Niceta, and their
names at first were, one Faustus, and the other Faustinianus.'
And when Peter said this, and named them by their names, the
old man was bewildered, and fainted, and his sons fell upon him
kissing him and weeping, supposing that he was dead. And the page 33

people were bewildered by this marvel, and Peter commanded us to lean off from the old man, and he took him by the hand, and raised him, and he related to the people all the misfortunes that had befallen him, and the reason that they happened.  And when our mother learned this, she came hurrying, crying and saying, 'Where is my husband and lord Faustinianus, who has been miserable on account of me for a long time, seeking me in every city?'  And while she was crying thus, the old man sprang hastily towards her with tears, and they embraced one another.  And after all this Peter sent away the crowd of people, and commanded them to come the next day and hear the story.  And behold, a man of the nobles came with his wife and children to ask us to go to his house, and Peter did not accept that from him.

page 34    And thereupon, behold, [there was] a daughter of the man [who had been] struck by a devil who had possessed her for twenty years, and on that account she was bound with chains, imprisoned in a house; the house was opened suddenly, and the chains were broken, and the devil came out from her; and the girl came and did obeisance to Peter, and said, 'O lord, I have come to thee to-day on account of my salvation, and do not grieve me nor my father.'  And Peter asked them about the girl, and her parents were bewildered when they saw the chains fallen from her, and her request to Peter.  And Peter had pity on her, and commanded us to go to his house.  And on the morrow our father came to us, and did all that Peter commanded him; and we turned the discourse so that there might be certainty in the controversy, and after very much page 35 speech in reproof of folly, Peter commanded our father not to dwell for any time on what is not necessary to God in religion, but that he should repent, for the end of life is near not only to old men, but also to young ones.  And he exhorted the old man with all the people for some days, then he baptized the old man in the name of the Father, and of the Son, and of the Holy Ghost, to whom be glory and praise for ever and ever, Amen.

O [thou] who readest, pray for him who wrote it.

The Lord remember thee in mercy, Amen, and all believers.

# RECOGNITIONS OF CLEMENT.

[*From a MS. in the British Museum*, No. XXVIII. (Add. 9965).]

THE story of our father, glorious amongst the saints, Clement
Pope of Rome, Martyr amongst the priests. This Blessed
Clement was from the great city of Rome, his family being
of the race of the Emperors, very learned and wise, as his
sayings and writings bear evidence, for he was educated in all
the wisdom of the Greeks, and he became a wonderful philo-
sopher. His father's name was Fafestus, and his mother's name
was Mattidian. He wrote the Canons of the Apostles and
other things; became bishop at Rome, and was banished by the
Emperor Domitian. But come, let us bring forward a little of
the much which this Blessed Clement expounded from that
which he wrote to James the Lord's Brother in the letter in
which he related to him minutely about all his affairs, and how
he turned from his former error to the knowledge of God.
Let us write this briefly together with his Martyrdom; for thus
it was written in the beginning of his letter: Know, O my lord
James, that I was born and bred in Rome, and I preserved
virginity from my youth, constantly remembering death; and
for this reason I was in much sadness, thinking thus inwardly
and saying, "Dost thou suppose that the soul of man is
immortal? Is there another world than this present one?"
With these and such like thoughts I studied night and day, and
my life passed thus in indescribable perplexity, and many
times I went to the dwellings of the philosophers, and asked
them about these things, that I might learn the truth. Some of
them said to me that the soul is immortal, and others of them

said the opposite of that, and some of them said also other things; and my soul was firmly determined to know the truth. I sought also from the wise men that I might know if there is in this universe torment, and Tartarus, and the Gehenna of fire, in which the wicked are punished after death, and if there is everlast-

f. 188 b ing rest to the good, that I might pass my life virtuously in this present world, and not be tormented yonder for ever.   I had in my heart an unappeasable longing like this.   I heard that in the land of Judæa there had appeared a great Prophet, perfect in holiness, a chief of the Jews, that He was proclaiming about the kingdom of God, teaching the people their salvation, and doing marvellous miracles: for He was giving sight to the blind, restoring the lame, raising the dead, and doing great wonders like these, preaching that all those who live virtuously in this present world shall go to the kingdom of the heavens.   When I heard this, I rejoiced greatly, and I hoped that I should learn what I longed for.   This [man's] praise was growing and being confirmed every day, until a man came from Jerusalem to us in Rome, and stood in the midst of the market-place, and spoke thus to the crowd, "Oh men, people of Rome, know that to-day the Son of God is found in the body in Jerusalem, and He promises to all who obey Him, and keep the commandments of God, and walk virtuously despising present things, that they shall enjoy enduring things, and eternal life.  They must know that the Trinity is one God.   He commands all dwellers in the world that they do no wrong inwardly, and that they all repent of their sins, that they may not be cast into the fire that shall not be quenched, and remain in it altogether without intermission." When I heard this sweet announcement, I rejoiced greatly and my soul exulted.   I left immediately all the cares of the world.  I found a boat, I entered it, and resolved to go to Jerusalem, that I might enjoy what I was longing for, and hear the truth from His lips.  When we were travelling, an adverse wind overtook us and hindered us; we arrived at Alexandria, and there I enquired about what had been announced to me. I heard from many that all that had been said about Him concerning these miracles and others was true. At that time there was an honoured disciple there named Barnabas ; he was much esteemed, being superior to all the teachers in these regions, so thereupon I went to him immediately and I found him teaching the people publicly, speaking about the miracles of Jesus the Christ, not in pride and boastfulness, but in humility and poverty. He was telling them many truths. And the philosophers were making game of him, and teaching people to ask him about what was not to the purpose ; but he was teaching on behalf of the Christ, and giving them answers. Thereupon I chased them away, and snatched Barnabas from the midst, that they might not do him any hurt. I took him to my house, and I fell down before his feet, begging him that he would relate to me the things of the Christ minutely, and that he would tell me the whole of the truths. I resolved that I would go with him to Jerusalem, for in those days he had determined that he would be there at the feast of the Passover, on account of the agreement that he had made with the rest of the Apostles ; but as for me, I had urgent affairs, and I could not go along with him. But I promised him that after a few days I should find him there. I did so, I went to Jerusalem, and I found him with Peter. They both rejoiced when they saw me ; then I had an interview with Peter, and I asked him to solve all the doubts which I had about the soul, whether it is mortal or immortal, and the rest of the things that were in my mind about what had been related to me. The Apostle at once explained to me all the truths, answered me [with] all wisdom the rest of my questions, and cured my mind by wonderful speeches. He shewed me the secret of the Holy Trinity, of His creation of the world, and of the incarnation of Jesus the Christ, that He is the Son and the Word, that the dead shall rise in the last day, and that there shall be a reward to the righteous and to sinners. He urged me to attain to holy baptism, that I might be planted with the Lord the Christ, so that I might rise and be glorified with Him in the heavenly and eternal kingdom, that I might have no doubt about future blessedness. He said to me in the

f. 189 a

f. 189 b   whole of these speeches of his " It is of necessity that the soul is
immortal, since God is by His nature just and of transcendent
integrity, and that He repay the righteous of mankind when
they rise, that every one of them may enjoy that which he
deserves on account of his work ; to the good [there shall be]
perfect rest, and everlasting joy, and to the wicked sorrows and
torments without end ; and all who have denied this and have not
believed in it are persuaded that God is unjust in neglecting the
true worshippers, the virtuous who are patient under manifold
griefs in this world and unspeakable torments and who die a
bitter death, as He does not reward them with enjoyment
on account of their good works ; but heretics and transgressors
of the law who have passed all their life in pleasure and
diversions and at the end die a good death, He does not punish
them in Gehenna on account of the evil of their deeds."   Then
he said to me afterwards that Simon Magus would inherit
eternal fire.   And when I heard these sayings from him, I felt
assured that all that he preached to me was truth, and I begged
the Saint to baptize me, and he told me that I must fast and
wash for three months, that I might be cleansed from all pains,
and then " thou shalt be worthy of divine baptism."   Some days
after that I heard that Peter would have a contest in public
with Simon Magus, and I asked one of Peter's disciples, whose
name was Aquila, about Simon Magus, and what manner [of
man] he was.   And he answered, " This Simon possesses
all the work of the Devil, for he deceives the people, and
performs tricks as if they were miracles, so that those present
are astonished at them, for he goes into the fire and is not burnt
and he appears like an eagle flying in the air, and he makes the
stones bread and they eat them, and he becomes a serpent or a
goat, or gold, or he is clothed in some other form, and he opens
closed doors, and he melts iron, and makes it like wax, and he

f. 190 a   creates utensils and house furniture, and calls on them to walk of
their own accord and serve their masters.   And this unrighteous
[man] does other sorceries."   When Aquila had told me about
this, there came a man named Zacchæus, and said to Peter, " Lo,

all the crowd has assembled, Simon is sitting on the chair, armed like a warrior, and they are all expecting to hear your dispute." Thereupon Peter commanded me to withdraw, as I was unbaptized, that he and the Apostles might offer solemn prayers that the Lord might help them, that Simon might be reclaimed from ignorance, and above all in the dispute with Simon for many hours. And when Peter conquered him, he could not bear [it] but he fled ashamed to the city of Tyre, and performed his sorceries there. Peter learned this, and sent Aquila and me, that we should go to Tyre, investigate about Simon, and write him the answer. So we went and alighted at the house of the Canaanitish woman, Bernice, daughter of Justa, according as Peter had commanded us. And they two received us with joy, and honoured us, and related to us about Simon, that he was performing his sorceries there according to his wont, till the senseless thought him a God; thus we wrote and sent to Peter, and he came at once. When Simon heard of his arrival he fled to another country, and he did not wait for his public dispute. And the Apostle Peter staid there for some days, and did many miracles, that he might save the people from the error of Simon, and thus, by the help of God, the greater number of them should be restored to the know-ledge of God. Then he passed from thence to the sea-side, and went to Tripolis, and appointed a bishop over Tripolis, whose name was Marouta. We then went out from thence to go to Antioch in Syria, and Peter sent Aquila and Niceta that they might first go before us, and that our travelling-companions might not be numerous, that those of the heathen who should see us might not be suspicious of us; and I rejoiced greatly when he kept me with him, and I was ready for all his service, so he said to me, "I am grateful for thy good service and thy management, but thou must know that I do not require various eatables, but only bread and oil, and sometimes herbs; and I do f. 190 b not possess a second dress, as thou seest, for all my mind is in the perfect goods for whose sake I despise every possession of present things with my whole soul and to the uttermost, for I was born of humble folk, and we were brought up orphans and poor, I and my brother Andrew; we had not much possession, and for that reason I am accustomed to poverty, enduring privations, in travel and other bodily miseries." After he had thus made me his companion, he asked me about my parents, what they were called, and what they were named, and he commanded me to tell him about their family and their names exactly. So I related it truthfully to him, saying, "My father was called Fafestus, he was prominent among the people of Rome, and for that reason Cæsar the Emperor gave him a wife of his own family, who was called Mattidia, and he begat from her twin sons, and he called their names Fafestinus and Fafestinianus; and after them he begat me, but I did not know my mother at all, for some time after she gave me birth, my mother saw at last a dream, as my father told me, that if she did not flee with her twin children to another country, we should all die. So my father put my mother with her sons into a boat and gave them much goods, and an escort, and slaves, and other necessary things, and sent them to Athens that the boys might learn letters; but he kept only me with him to console him. And after a year he sent to my mother, with some people, silver to Athens for maintenance, and these people also did not return. So in the third year he sent others, and they came back to him in the fourth year, and said to him that they had not found my mother nor my brothers nor their companions. And my father was very sorrowful, and he put his office in charge, and left me and Rome and everything, and went into a boat to seek my mother and my brothers and those who were with him. But from that time he did not return, and did not send us a letter at all and I think that on account of his many griefs for them death f. 191 a  has overtaken him, or he has been drowned in the sea. And it is now twenty years that I have not heard news of him." When Peter heard this, he began to weep, like one bereaved, and he said to those who were with us in the boat, "Know, my dear friends, that when griefs and afflictions assail believers, they are patient under them, knowing that on account of them they deserve the pardon of their sins, and they shall attain to everlasting joy on account of their present grief; whereas miserable heathens both endure affliction here, and after death also they shall be afflicted on account of their infidelity in the punishment that has no end." And when Peter preached this to us, we saw an island before us, called Aradus. And some of its people begged Peter to come into it for a little rest, and he obeyed them. And this was by the guidance of God that I might find my mother there. When we got out on the island, each went where he liked, and Peter, by the guidance of God, went round many ways. And a poor woman turned to him, and begged alms from him. And he said to her, "Why, O woman, dost thou not work with thy hands, and nourish thyself by thy labour? yet thou seekest thy food from others." And she answered, "I have somewhat in the form of hands, O my Lord, but they are paralysed and useless, and I cannot do the least service with them." Then she wept and heaved a great sigh. And Peter was grieved in sympathy with her weeping, and begged her to tell him about her misfortune and her grief, so she said to him, "I am of a great family in Rome, and I had a husband illustrious in power, and three male children. But when my husband's brother saw my beauty, he wished to persuade me to adultery, and I had a great longing for chastity, for it is an honourable thing, and I fled from my country, that my husband might not know this thing, and kill me and his brother together, and I should be the cause. So thus I told a lie to my husband, that I had seen a dream that I should travel with my two sons, that we might not die all of us. So he sent me to Athens that our sons might learn literature in books; and when we were travelling by sea, there came on us during the last night a great commotion in the sea, and our boat was wrecked, and every one in it was drowned, excepting poor unfortunate me. I took hold of the rudder, and by its means f. 191 b I got to the land; and I was trembling and half-dead. When day came, I searched for my boys and did not find them. And some peasants came and found me naked; and they clothed

me, and comforted me, and brought me to this village ; and a
poor widow woman took me to her house. Every day she
comforted me, saying that her husband had been a sailor and
had been drowned in the sea, and I, from the greatness of my
grief and the trembling of my hands had taken a staff in my
hands ; and on this side I am bewitched ; and this woman who
received me is in great weakness, and is lying paralysed in her
house ; she cannot move, and there is nothing for us to live
upon except a little alms which people give us, and we live
in great privation together." And when Peter heard her speech,
he knew that she was my mother, and he asked her, saying,
"What were thy husband and children called, and what were their
names ?" and she said unto him, "My husband was called Fafestus,
and my sons were Fafestinus and Fafestinianus, and the little one
was called Clement," and she finished her narrative. And Peter
said to her by the guidance of God, "Hail, O woman ! for in this
very day thou shalt see thy son." And he commanded her that
she should not make a disturbance till we should get away from
the island. Then he took hold of her hand, and brought her to
the boat. And when I saw how Peter was leading the woman, I
smiled, not knowing the reason, and I went to meet him, and do
him honour, and take his hand ; and Peter said to her, " This is
Clement," and she embraced me and kissed me, weeping. But
I was very angry, as I did not know the reason, so Peter said to
me, "Let thy mother have pleasure in thee." When I heard
this, I wept, and fell down to kiss her feet. All the by-
standers were astonished at me, that I was rich and eloquent,
and the son of great people, and my mother thus in poverty in a
measure. We wished to go away from that island, so Peter said
to my mother that she should go into the boat and travel with us.
And she answered him, " I beg of thee, O my lord, to allow me
f. 192a first to go and take leave of my companion, for she received me
for the Lord's sake, and entertained me according to her means,
when the poor woman was in health, and now she is bed-ridden
and paralysed." Peter admired the beauty of my mother's
resolution. And he commanded, and they brought the paralysed

woman before him, and he spoke thus to her in the hearing of all, "If I have been preaching the truth, stand up whole, that these present may believe that the one God created all the world," and for the sake of God by a miracle the paralysed woman stood up, and became entirely whole, and did homage to the physician, and thanked him for his kindness, as was fitting. When my mother saw this miracle, she was astonished as well as all the rest of the by-standers, and she begged Peter that he would cure her also. Then Peter put his hand on her, and she was cured immediately. Thereupon my mother thanked the Apostle, and I paid a thousand dirhems in silver to the chief man in the island, because they had received my mother among them, and I commanded him to distribute them in alms, by reason of my love for the poor and the deserving, and we travelled together with my mother, after that Peter had baptized the woman who had received her and others, and all those who believed in the teaching of the Apostle, and we went from thence in circuit from one country to another, till we arrived at Laodicæa where Aquila and Niceta met us and received us as was fitting to stranger-guests. When Peter saw the greatness of this city and the multitude of its people, he resolved to stay there many days, that he might preach the word of faith. Thereupon Niceta and Aquila asked me about my mother, saying, "Who and whence is this woman your companion?" Then Peter told them her story from its beginning to its end. When they heard his speech, they remained astonished for many hours, and after that they cried thus with tears, saying, "We are her sons Fafestinus and Fafestinianus, the brothers of Clement." Then they related before their mother all that had happened to them with the sailors, saying, "Our boat was wrecked, and immediately there was a boat beside us in which were pirates. f. 192 b They took us with them in their boat, and went with us to Cæsarea Philippi, and changed our names and sold us. A well educated and very rich woman bought us, named Justa. She loved us as her own sons, and brought us up in all the knowledge of the Greeks, and when we grew older, behold, we were taught philo-

sophy also, that we might preach and teach the heathen, to lead
them to the true faith.   We desired to learn the deceitfulness and
vanities of idols.   After that we met with a man called Simon,
for he imagined he would deceive us according to his polluted
determination, but by the doing of God we made friends with
one of the disciples of the Christ, called Zacchæus, and he
taught us to leave Simon; he led us to Peter, the Apostle of
the Lord, and he exhorted us and baptized us.   Thus we pray
God that He would count thee worthy also of holy baptism."
When they had related this, they embraced my mother, weeping
with copious tears and joyfulness.   Thereupon I sought from the
Apostle Peter that I might attain to holy baptism.   He commanded me also to fast for the same number of days as those
who were fasting diligently.   We implored him to baptize us,
for we had eaten nothing since the time that we entered the
boat; as my mother testified.   We implored him also to baptize
us that we might eat bread with her, that we might rejoice in
spirit, for I was not baptized, and I had not eaten at one table
with them all.   But Peter, that he might not sin before God, as
he was a Saint, and that he might also fulfil our desire, commanded us to fast along with him, all that day and the next,
that we might be worthy of holy baptism, and thus he did.
And after our baptism Peter took bread, and blessed and
sanctified the bread, and brake it, and gave it first to my
mother, and afterwards to us, and we eat, rejoicing and glorifying God.   And after that an old man came to us and spoke thus
to Peter, " Do not be deceived, O man, and do not pray, for God
has no existence, and there is no Providence of God, but only a
f. 193 a Fortune to every man, and all that is destined to happen to a
man, good or bad, he enjoys it whether he prays or does not
pray, as I know from experience; for I was very well off, and
much respected, and I did good to the poor by much alms, that
the gods might help me, and that no sorrow might attack me
from anything that was destined to happen to me.   But the gods
could not keep me without misfortune."   This and more than
this the old man said to Peter.   But Peter contradicted his

speech, and shewed him the truth, saying that there is one God only, who is immortal, and who has foreordained all things in His just wisdom, and some of them by His forbearance; and afterwards Peter asked him to tell him whence he was, and what trials had befallen and happened to him. He answered him, saying, " I was among the grandees of Rome, well-versed in the art of astrology and I married a woman of the family of Cæsar the Emperor, and I begat three boys of her, and it was written against her in her fate that she was to become corrupt, for she loved one of her slaves; and when she could not abide the judgement of people about her, she fled with him to another country. She took with her the older boys, and left the youngest with me, and lo! she married this slave, and thus she died with her sons. But my young boy remained in my house, and at last I went to seek the woman and her sons, and my young boy was lost also, and here am I going about from place to place, and I cannot return to my home on account of my confusion, and I now get my food by much toil and moil." When Peter heard that, he knew that the old man was my father in truth, and he asked him about his name, and about the name of his wife and his sons. He answered him, " My name is Fafestus, and my wife is Matthidia, and my sons Fafestinus and Fafestini-anus, and the young one Clement." Thereupon I wept, and Peter, and therewith I went to my mother and announced to her that I f. 193 b had found my father, her husband. She went out crying and weeping and seeking him, and when she recognized him she remained for many hours silent from excess of joy as if she were dead. Then we three boys came and did obeisance to our father and we said to him, " We are thy sons." All that day we had indescribable joy, and we thanked the All-powerful God who had thought us worthy to enjoy one another. Afterwards, behold, Peter held discussion with my father, and exhorted him to believe in the Christ, forbidding him to talk such nonsense as he had done at first, and to believe that God is true, "and in the fulness of His wisdom He foreordained that these mis-fortunes should come upon you, and that the boat should be

wrecked, and that you should be parted from each other, that
after these sorrows that befel you, you should come together
again, and be enlightened in the true faith." At length by much
exhortation and plain teaching my father knew the truth, and
came to true worship.   When he believed in the Christ and was
baptized, he was filled with divine zeal, so he took leave of
Peter, and went to dispûte with Simon Magus, for he was in
Antioch at that time.   When Simon saw that my father looked
like a magician in the eyes of the people, that unrighteous one
made an exchange, and began to be disguised and shew his
devilish tricks, and my father also began to be disguised and to
work and make himself as if he were Simon Magus.   Then the
infidel Simon made his form like the form of my father, because
the Emperor had sent troops from Rome to seize Simon and
bring him bound to Rome as he was a seducer and magician, and
kill him according to his deserts.   So the deceiver, that he might
escape from this misfortune, disguised himself in the form of my
father, that they might kill him instead of Simon; but Simon
fled to the land of Judæa and was absent.   Then afterwards
when our father came from Antioch to us, and we beheld him
like Simon, we were astonished.   Then Peter heard from the
Antiochenes that Simon was teaching all the people of Antioch
f. 194 a his godlessness and inciting them to kill the Apostle Peter when
he went to them, as a seducer and a deceiver, and they were
now all prepared to fulfil the saying of Simon.   When Peter
heard that, he sent my father with my two brothers and my
mother and other people, that they should go to Antioch, saying
to my father, "Go now, O Fafestus, to Antioch, and shew the
form of Simon, and preach to the crowd as from his mouth, that
they may know the truth, and believe that God is in truth one
and eternal, and such like."   So my father went joyfully to
Antioch, according to Peter's command to him, and he stood in
the midst of the city and called thus: "Know, O people of Antioch,
that we wronged Peter when we suspected him, for this man is a
Saint, and I have accused him falsely in vain ; but now I beg you
to receive him when he comes and to believe and trust in his teach-

ing, for he is the Apostle of the true God who never lies, and do all that he commands you. If you do not thus to him, he will destroy you all and your city together. I came for this purpose to give you news, lest you should do evil to him, for angels appeared to me last night and beat me as in truth an infidel and hater of warning, so I beg this of you. Know this also, that I came to you the other time, and I deceived you by the working of the devil, and I made a wicked speech about Peter, so do not trust me, for I confess to-day publicly before you that I am a seducer and a magician, but now I have returned to repentance, in hope that God will forgive my sins." When my father spoke thus to the Antiochenes from the face of Simon and blessed and praised Peter, he immediately changed the mind of all the Antiochenes, who had formerly hated the Apostle, and made them love him, my father sent us word to come there that he might enjoy the sweetness of Peter's exhortation. I immediately went with Peter and the rest of our companions. All the Antiochenes received him with great joy as a true prophet and an Apostle of God. He prayed, f. 194 b and put his right hand upon the sick, and cured them all; and he taught a great crowd to believe in God, the Trinity in persons, and he confirmed the true faith. Then my father fell at Peter's feet, imploring him to make him a Christian, and perfect him by holy baptism, that he might return to his previous form, and attain to the divine mysteries. So Peter commanded him to weep and fast till the morrow, and on the second day he exhorted him much and many others, and taught them how to walk in the orthodox faith blameless; and he baptized them in the name of the Father and of the Son and of the Holy Ghost; and he afterwards stayed there many days teaching the Antiochenes. And we all suffered many trials from the devil, the enemy of the truth. When the Governor heard that we were of the family of Cæsar the Emperor, he sent to inform the Emperor Tiberius of this. The Emperor, when he knew it, sent to say to him to send my father and mother to Rome quickly. The Governor gave them great gifts, and honoured them much, and sent them. When the Emperor saw my father and mother, he wept much from the excess of his joy, and he fell upon their necks, kissing them, and he spoke thus to the rest of his lords: "Rejoice with me, all of you, this day, and come, let us make a public feast for our finding of Fafestus and Matthidia; for we supposed them dead, and they have risen, and lost, and they are found." He made them a great table, and eat with them. Then he gave them much gold, and slaves, and guards, and other splendid gifts, because of the nobility of their race, that they might live according to their former custom. And behold they were known in Rome for their virtues and true worship, keeping the faith of the Christ immovable. At last they distributed the whole of their goods among the poor, and fulfilled all good works, and completed their lives in what was pleasing to God. They forsook present things, and they inherited heavenly things. But I and my brothers did not part from our Teacher Peter at all, but we were continually with him, in obedience to him and in his travels; we bore with him all sorrows and sufferings of various kinds from the infidels in the towns and villages when we went to preach the Gospel. At last we arrived at famous Rome, and Peter preached in it publicly about the Christ, and wrought many miracles, and turned many to the faith, and baptized them, not only among the humble, but many rich folk, and women of the imperial house, among whom was the Mistress of the Ceremonies. Now when Peter resolved to go to the Christ our Teacher, he saw a divine vision, that after a few days he should be crucified, that he might become a sharer in the pains of his Lord. So he collected all the brethren, and stood in the midst of the church, and took my hand and spoke thus to the crowd: "Know this, O my brethren and my children, that I have arrived at the end of my life, inasmuch as my Lord the Christ has appeared to me, and behold, I appoint Bishop over you this my disciple Clement, and I establish him upon the chair as your Shepherd from to-day; for he has been a sharer in all my trials and griefs

f. 195 a

which we endured, and I know him that he is a servant of God
who loves men; pure and chaste, good, true, and long suffering,
so he will be patient in griefs and other hostile things which
will come to him.  For this reason I give him power to loose
and to bind whatever is necessary, for he knows the canons of
the church very well.  You must all be submissive to him, for
whosoever murmurs against the true chief is angry with God,
and shall inherit the death and the torments of rebels.  The
leader too must be like the true physician, and not be angry and
passionate for want of knowledge."  When Peter spoke thus, I  f. 195 b
fell at his feet, excusing myself from the headship.  He said to
me, "Do not oppose the will of God, O my son."  He turned to
the crowd, and commanded them all to walk in faith in all
purity and blamelessness, to love one another; and if one happens
to be vexed or angry with another, let him make friends with
him before the sun goes down.  Let them not judge any one,
but pardon whomsoever has sinned against them, that God may
forgive and pardon them their sins.  Then he commanded them
all also to shew me great respect, as the respect they had shewn to
him; and when he had exhorted them with these and other like
exhortations, he sat in the chair and said to me, "I beg thee to
write to James the Lord's brother after my death and exodus
from life all that has happened to thee since thy youth and
what has happened to us in our journeys until this day and my
departure, and the completion of my testimony, and how I
have glorified God by my death, being crucified, as the Lord
has borne me company.  For when he hears this, he shall attain
to great joy and consolation."  But I Clement, that I might
respond to the command of my teacher Peter, have written to
thee, O my lord James, and have sent to thee briefly all that
has happened to me.  Do thou pray for me to the Lord that
he may count worthless me worthy to tend what has been
entrusted to me with a care well-pleasing to God, and that I
may end my life by martyrdom.

# STORY OF THE MARTYRDOM OF
## SAINT CLEMENT.

THUS far is the letter of this Blessed Clement, which he wrote with his hand to the Apostle James, from which every one can understand the greatness of his love to the Lord and his zeal for the true faith, so that he may know still further from the end of this Blessed one by martyrdom, for he experienced in it a threefold blessedness with courage that he might glorify the Lord and strengthen the true faith, inasmuch as he was a good

disciple to Peter and worthy of the succession to his chair, for he was like his Teacher in virtues with good habits and exertions and other virtues. He was a teacher to the Jews and the Gentiles, and he was with every one like every one that he might gain all to stand in true worship to the Christ. He was very humble, sweet in his address and his exhortation, so that the Greeks and the Jews had a great love and respect for him, for he did not shew himself stern and fault-finding, but explained to them with great humility and gentleness the evidences from their books, that his speech might be worthy of his trust. He did not upbraid any of them and did not neglect them at all; to the ignorant he explained about their idols one by one what and who they were, and he explained to them their contemptible character and he taught for what reason they imagined them gods. At the end of his exhortation he continually preached about the greatness of the pity of the true God, and the fulness of His mercy; he incited them to repentance and promised them that the kingdom of heaven should be open to those of them who returned on condition only that they should desist from their former sins, believe in the Christ, and be baptized; and that God would receive them. As for the Jews, he praised them in the beginning of his discourse, saying that they were the chosen people of God, because they were of the race of Abraham, and such like praises, and at the end he did honour to the New Testament and he did not despise the Old one, so that they might not doubt; but he finished his speech with wisdom and thus he wrought much profit to many, guiding and leading every one by his discourse to the true faith. He took care also of the organization of the Christians continually, undertaking the affairs of the poor, that none of the necessaries of the body might be wanting to them, neither to men nor to widow women nor to orphans belonging to the city. He wrote them all down in a register, and he gave each of them alms in suitable measure to carry on his life. Thus did the pitiful Clement, in mercy like the Christ. All the Emperor's Court honoured and respected him, except one of them, whose name was Socinius. He f. 196 b related much to the Emperor Nero. This man hated him, and told the Emperor of his own invention how Clement had converted his wife Theodora from the worship of the idols, and that she was not now attending to her house or her children, but was continually going to the church of the Christians to learn their doctrines. This hatred was in the heart of Socinius, and he was armed every day with the armour of iniquity and jealousy and envy lurking in his heart towards the Saint. He designed evil against his wife Theodora when he should find a convenient season, and one day he acted treacherously. There was a gathering of the Christians, so he went and hid himself in the church with his slaves to see what his wife was doing there. When he arrived at the church, the Saint was praying at the moment, and immediately Socinius remained blind and deaf. He said to his slaves, "Take me and lead me that I may go to my house, for blindness and deafness have come suddenly upon me, and behold, I neither see nor hear at all." The slaves led him by his hand, and wished to try and go out of the church, and they could not; but they went round here and there without avail, for the Divine Power prevented them, that this senseless [man] might be educated and punished. When Theodora saw him thus, she asked the reason of it. They told her his story, and she implored the Lord with tears to be gracious to him about going out, and it was so. His slaves brought him to his house, and put him to bed blind and deaf by the act of God. When Theodora returned to her house, they told her his story in detail. She was grieved, and shewed kindness to him, and went and fell at the Saint's feet, imploring with tears that he would cure her husband. So Clement went to the house of the sick man, and wept over him, and implored God, praying for him and saying, "O Lord Jesus the Christ, Thou who hast given the keys of Thy kingdom to Thy Apostle Peter that he may open and shut to whom he wills, open Thou the eyes and the ears of this man, for thou hast promised us to give us along with Thy salvation all our petitions." When the Saint prayed thus for the sick [man] he was immediately cured of his bodily blindness, and heard with his bodily ears, but his soul remained still in the former error. He imagined that the Saint was a wizard, and did these things by his enchantments, and the blind sight of the poor [man] was just as at first in error. So the thankless one commanded his servants to seize the Saint at that time and to bind him, that he might repay him for his grace by its opposite. But the servants seized wood and stones, thinking they were the Saint, and bound them, for they were bewildered by Divine retribution. Socinius thought that his slaves had bound the Saint, and he boasted against him, saying to him, "Thus, O Clement, I make vain quickly thy sorceries and thy deceit that thou mayest be educated." But the Saint was preserved un-bound, and came forward and said to him, "Thus, O senseless [man], thy heart has been blind, O miserable being; do not think that thou bindest me ; but I bind thy gods whom thou worshippest from the first," and he left him despised and humbled. Then the Saint blessed Theodora and commanded her to pray to God without ceasing for her husband, that he might turn to the true worship, and she prayed, imploring God for him with tears, and in the evening there appeared to her a venerable man with a white beard, in the likeness of Peter

f. 197 a

the Apostle, and said to her, "For thy sake I have cured thy
husband, in order that the husband may be sanctified by the
wife, as my brother Paul the Apostle commanded." When he
spoke thus to her, he departed immediately, and Socinius, by
the act of Divine grace, called his wife, and said to her, "I
believe in my Lord Jesus the Christ, the only true God, to
whom I have prayed that He would forgive me my former
follies, and secondly wilt thou mediate for me with Saint
Clement, that he may not feel angry with me the thankless
one, inasmuch as he is a disciple of God, that he may have f. 197 b
compassion on me?" When the woman heard that, she rejoiced
and wept, and she at once told that to the good [man]. He
hastened at once and came to the house of Socinius, who
received him with much humility, and fell at his feet weeping
passionately and said to him with a contrite heart, "I thank the
true God and thy Holiness because thou didst blind my bodily
eyes and enlighten my soul, that I might know the truth and
flee from the error of the Greeks and their falsehood, for with
my whole heart I have accepted warning in the true faith."
It was then the feast of Easter, so there was then a great
festival in that house, and Socinius and all his people were
baptized, and his friends and his slaves, both men and women,
and their number was 423 persons, and there were many
among them who were friends and acquaintances of the Emperor.
But when Publius the (director?) of all saw this, he was
grieved that the faith was then growing and increasing, so he
took it into his head to kill the Saint who was the cause of all
these things; and he paid silver to some people, and agreed
with them that they should make a commotion with the
Governor of the city and accuse the Saint before him, that they
might incite him to kill him speedily; and these people came
to the Governor and accused the Saint as a seducer and a
wizard, that he blasphemed the gods, and destroyed their
temples from the foundations, and worshipped a new god, and
built churches and altars to him in every place. Then those
who had not received bribes praised the Saint before the Gover-

nor, telling of the miracles and the good works which he did to all the city. When the Governor saw the greatness of the talk and commotion of the crowd he called the Saint secretly, and tried him with many flatteries that he should return to his error. When he saw that he was firm and bold and unshaken, he sent news of him before the Emperor Tiberius, saying to him that there had been a great commotion in the city on account of Clement. The Emperor decided about him that they should banish him to a desert town which is in the borders of the Chersonesus. The Governor grieved about the Saint because he was destined to go

f. 198 a  to this bitter exile. He sent for him, and commanded him to offer the mid-day sacrifice to the idols, and not go into this exile. The Saint wished by the eloquence and sweetness of his accents to convert the Governor to faith in the Christ. When the Governor saw the Saint's want of submission, he dismissed him, sighing and weeping, saying to him, " The God whom thou servest, he will help thee in this hard exile." He then provided him with all his necessaries, and sent him in a boat, and embraced and kissed him, and sent him away. Many conscientious men followed him into exile. He found there some thousands of Christians, oppressed and previously exiled, who were cutting marble there. When they saw the Saint, they rejoiced much ; they did homage to him, kissed his hands respectfully, and told him their mis-fortune and privation, and their want of even what was most necessary ; worse than all that, they had no water to slake their thirst by reason of their work and fatigue and the greatness of their misery ; but they had been going and fetching the water from a far place, at a distance of 45 bow-shots. The Saint had pity on them, weeping; then he comforted them much, saying to them, " It is the will of God that we should be exiled, and should be sharers in torments and sufferings." When he said this, he commanded them all to make solemn prayer together with him, imploring Almighty God to give them water as He is pitiful. When the Saint had finished his prayer, he looked here and there, and saw from afar a lamb lifting its right foot and pointing to the earth before it ; no one saw the lamb save the

Saint. He went with three men, and said to them, " Dig this place where the lamb was standing." When they had made a little hole, the good [man] took the axe with his hand and dug a little with it, and spoke thus, " In the name of our Lord Jesus the Christ, let fresh sweet water rise in this place." When he had spoken thus, what miracles are thine, O Christ, the Almighty King! immediately water flowed out there copiously, f. 198 b and formed a great stream, and there was sweet delicious water. The Saint took some of it and drank, and thus they all drank rejoicing. On account of this miracle the people of the villages there honoured the Saint and reverenced him, and they hastened to him on all occasions and heard the sweetness of his teaching. He converted innumerable people amongst them to true worship, and baptized them in the name of the Holy Trinity; he destroyed the idol-temples and built churches for them; for in the course of years from his stand-point there the Saint built for believers 75 churches; he burnt and razed all the idols, and abolished all traces of them. When the Emperor learned [this], he sent to Aphidianus the governor to agitate on every side, so as to do away with the faith of the Christ. So the Governor persecuted many of the Christians there with divers punishments. When he saw that they were all desirous to be martyrs for the sake of the Christ, and were prepared for that, he took it into his head to kill the Saint who was the cause of that; so he put upon the Blessed Clement the hardest punishments, and persecuted him much. When he saw that he was the more desirous of martyrdom, and that he strengthened and confirmed the believers, he condemned him to death, that they should bind on his neck a thick boat-rope, and throw him into the depths of the sea, that the believers might not find his honoured body. When they threw him into the sea, many of the Christians stood near the sea mourning and weeping for their teacher. Cornelius and Fifus his disciples cried with inconsolable grief and commanded the others all to pray to God in company, imploring Him to bring out the Saint's body to the earth. When they all prayed together, weeping, a great marvel took place, for once upon a time Moses accomplished a surprising miracle in the Red Sea, but here a miraculous wonder took place and was accomplished,

f. 199 a that the sea fled back twenty miles, and the Christians went forward on dry land. How surpassing is thy power, O Almighty Christ! They found a great hewn stone like a church, adjusted by wonderful art through the astonishing wisdom of God, and in its midst a splendid temple. There was the body of the honoured Saint laid out shining, and near that great heavy stone that coarse rope mentioned above. Cornelius and Fifus wished to lift the Saint, but they heard a celestial voice saying thus to them, " Leave [him] where the wonderful Lord has buried him." So they left him, and by this power till now every year in honour and remembrance of the Martyr the sea turns backward on the day of the commemoration of the Saint and stays thus for seven days, that the faithful may come and celebrate his holy feast. When the crowd heard this voice, they glorified God, and only kissed the Saint's body, and returned rejoicing. The miracle happened not at this time only, as well as other astonishing miracles, but every year in commemoration of this Saint the sea runs backward as we have mentioned, and gives the people time to celebrate the holy feast. At that time there were many other miracles, for all who went there and were sick of diseases and drank the water of that sea where was the temple of this Saint, were cured of all their sicknesses. After a few days, all the Christians who lived near that place went when they saw these miraculous wonders, but they heard a wonder greater than all these wonders, inasmuch as there was a believer who had great faith in this Saint. He went to worship the Saint in his temple above mentioned with his wife and his companions, and he had a little son. When their return was near, they stood in the temple of this Saint, praying that God would give their boy a long life and other things. When the sea was about to return to its place, the parents of the lad fled with others of the Christians with great

f. 199 b speed lest the sea should cover them; from fear and great confusion they left the lad there; they did not suppose that the water of the sea would cover him like the grave. Then when they sought him and found him not, they knew that he had remained in the temple of the Saint. They wept for him much and returned to their dwelling. When they saw his clothes also, their grief for him increased, and they were inconsolable. When this year had gone by, and the feast of this Saint came round, these [people] went to search lest they might find the bones of their son. When the sea turned back according to its custom every year, they hastened before every one to the temple of the Martyr. When they arrived there, they found their boy standing near the grave of the Saint. They at first doubted it, and thought it was a hallucination. When they looked at him well, and were sure he was their son, they hugged him and kissed him, and wept from the greatness of their joy. They asked him, "Whence have you got to eat this year, and how have you been kept from the sea-monsters without harm?" The boy pointed with his finger to the Saint and said, "He feeds me and protects me." Then the grief of his parents turned into joy, and they thanked God saying, "God is wonderful in His Saints," and such like things in praise of God. When they had finished the feast, they returned to their dwelling rejoicing, happy, and glorifying God, who had been doing His dread will and honouring them. The martyrdom of this Saint was on the 24th day of November, and we ask the Lord our God to grant us his mediation, and to count us with him in the kingdom of the Heavens, Amen.

Poor Macarius the Antiochene wrote it with his mortal hand, and translated it from the Greek language to the Arabic language, in the year 7167 of the world, corresponding to 1659 from the Incarnation of the Christ, on the 22nd of October, and it was written in the fortress-city of Sinope.

# THE PREACHING OF PETER.

IN the name of the Father, and of the Son, and of the Holy Ghost, one God.

This is the preaching of Simon Cephas, chief of the Disciples, and their leader, Peter, when the Christ, our Lord and our God, sent him to preach in the city of Rome.

God called Simon Cephas, and spoke to him, saying, "Simon, Simon, chief of the disciples, Rome wishes for thee; go out therefore to these people, whom the devil has led astray." And when Simon, the disciple of God, heard this, he began to weep before[1] God, and to say, "My God, whither shall I go, and I an aged man, I cannot walk, and I have neither gold nor silver, nor yet manners, how can I then go? I shall die like him who goeth to destruction. I desire of thee, O Lord, that thou wouldst pardon me, and cause me to die in Jerusalem[2], where Thy passion took place, I will then die at Thy word." And the Lord said unto Simon, "Do not begin to fear in thy heart. I give unto thee the power of the kingdom, therefore fear not, go, and enter among them. Fear not, speak to the sick, and they shall recover; say to the blind 'See,' and they shall see; and if they do not receive and take hold of thy word, they shall learn that I am in Heaven; therefore speak to the earth, and it shall swallow them up; and whatsoever thou shalt bind on earth, I will bind it in Heaven, and whatsoever thou shalt loose on the earth, I will loose it in Heaven. I am in Heaven, and thou art in the strange country. Thou shalt call to me from afar, and I will answer thee from at hand."

page 2

[1] Literally 'betwixt the hands of.'
[2] Or 'the holy house.'

And Simon said, "My God, forsake me not! I have trusted in Thee, and if thou forsakest me, I shall sink down to the lowest depth."

Then Simon stood up towards his brethren and his friends, with his tears flowing, and said, "Arise, my brethren, all of you, page 3 and call to mind the love which was between us, and abound in your prayers for me in this journey which God has given me; for like a dead man I go out from amongst you, therefore plead for me in your prayers."

And they said unto him, "Go in peace, O holy one, and may the God who is in Heaven be with thee, and the right hand which divided the sea before the children of Israel be with thee, O holy one of God, O pillar of the faith. Go, and may the angel of the Lord be with thee, and help thee upon thy way, and against thy enemy."

And Simon Peter crossed the sea until he came to the city of Rome. And they collected together when they saw him, and they began to say amongst themselves, "In truth this poor needy man has come. He is a seditious and weakly fellow, and he page 4 wears ragged clothes, and there are many poor people amongst us, but we never saw one like this one." And the beloved of God fell upon the dung-heap of a rich man, and he was hungry and thirsty, and the cold attacked him, and he had fallen on his face in great remembrance of God.

And the daughter of that rich man went out and looked at him; then she went in and said to her father, "O my father, there is an old man fallen down on our dunghill, like our old slave, and he is in our midst, and one of ourselves, and do bring him in and feed him with the bread that is in our dwelling." And her father answered and said unto her, "Go, my dear, as thou hast said, so be it, and cut short his prayer."

And the girl went out, and did him reverence, and said to him, "Arise, and do not weep, O my father, for thou hast already reached the house, so do not be grieved. Arise, and eat food, and throw care from off thee."

Then stood Simon, chief of the Disciples, with her, that she page 5 might set before him food to eat. And she put a chair for him, and he sat down; and she set vessels before him of silver and gold; then he asked water from her, and she went in haste, and came with a golden pot in her hand. And when she came near him she covered her hand.

And Simon said to her, "Tell me, O girl, why dost thou cover thy hand from me?"

And she said to him, "I was afflicted at the time of my going to my husband; and when my husband came to take me to the house of his family, and the golden crown was upon my head, behold, they shewed me in the market-places; and when I arrived at the house of my husband, this leprosy appeared in me. Thereupon I was ashamed before my companions, and I returned to my father's house. And I vowed a vow to our gods the idols, page 6 and I gave the great price, and I worshipped our heroes, but it is now six months since this disease appeared in me. And therefore I was ashamed, and I covered my hand, lest thou shouldst look at it."

And Peter took that pot of water, and prayed over it, with a conscience upright, acceptable, and spiritual (nothing of the carnal in it). Then Peter took that water-pot, and gave it to the girl, and said to her, "Wash thy body with this water." And when she washed her body with that water, she was cured and cleansed, and she became as though nothing had ever befallen her of that leprosy which she had. And when she saw that, she feared because of it with a great fear. Then she went to her father, who was a door-keeper, and she said to him, "O father, why dost thou sit still? Look at me!" And she uncovered her hand.

page 7 And when her father saw her cured of that leprosy which had appeared in her, he said to her, "Ah! my daughter, what is this which I see in thee this day?"

She said to him, "In truth I tell thee, O father, that the God of truth came in to us this day."

And her father the door-keeper went down to Peter, and said to him, "Cure for me the rest of my daughter's body from

that leprosy, and ask me what thou wilt of gold and silver that
I may give [it] thee." Peter said unto him, "I will cure the rest
of thy daughter's body from that leprosy, and I wish no gold
nor silver from thee, but I wish from thee a single word; that
thou wilt believe in my Lord Jesus the Christ, and that thou
wilt forsake the worship of idols and of devils whom we do not
worship."

And the door-keeper said unto Peter, "I give thee this[1]." And
Peter rose, and filled a font in that place where they were, and  page 8
Peter took the damsel, and dipped her in that font, and cleansed
her with that cleansing, and plunged her in that baptism in the
name of the Father, and of the Son, and of the Holy Ghost.
And she was cleansed from that leprosy which was in her as if
nothing had ever been formed in her at all (of that leprosy which
had been in her). And when her father the door-keeper saw
that, he believed in the Christ, and he left off the worship of
idols. Then Peter remained with them a day and a night; then
after that Peter wished to go out into the city of Rome and see
the people. And the door-keeper said to him, "If thou shouldst
go to-day to the city of Rome, thou canst not enter and go about
in its market-places, for they have a feast and vows, in which  page 9
they sacrifice to the idols, and if they see thee going about
among them in these rags, the gods will kill thee."

And Peter said to the door-keeper who believed in Christ,
" I cannot but go to the city of Rome, for my Lord Jesus the
Christ sent me as for this day and such as this, and I cannot
disobey my Lord." And Peter went away until he entered the
city of Rome, and behold, there were in it heralds proclaiming
and saying, " Let every person put on gowns and garments, and
gold and silver, and purple and pearls, and if not, let him blame
no one but himself." And the troops and their priests met Peter,
and said to him, " O foolish old man, where art thou going to-day
in these rags which are upon thee ? If the Emperor of Rome see  page 10
thee to-day he will kill thee. He who puts on raiment of gold
and silver, let him go up to the place of our gods." And Peter

---

[1] Literally ' This is thine from me.'

said, "O kings, and priests, and troops, this raiment is the raiment of my Lord, who gave [it] to me, He besides whom there is no god."

And they observed that saying, and they were angry at that with a great anger, and they commanded him to be stoned with stones for his speech about the Christ, that He is God.

And when Peter saw that, he came to the place of a temple, where their gods were, and he stood alone. Then he calleth on the Christ with an upright conscience, acceptable and spiritual, (nothing of the carnal was mingled with it in that place), and page 11 there the Emperor of Rome went out and many kings and troops, and thousands of priests innumerable, and with him a hundred girls, fifty of them married, and fifty who had never yet gone in to their husbands, and already they were taken and bound for the sacrifice, by a vow to their gods the idols and the devils whom they served, and when Peter saw that, he lifted up his eyes to heaven, and said, "My Lord, and my God, I cannot longer endure the thing which I have seen. But yet Thy mercy and Thy power is needed in an hour like this."

And the Christ answered Peter's prayer to Him, and He sent a great cloud and a stormy wind, and it threw down these idols and broke them ; and devils came out of them, and took refuge in the mountains. And when the Emperor of Rome saw that, he page 12 said to the girls, "Go to your parents;" and he said to the virgin fifty, "Go to your house, for my kingdom perishes by this darkness which is upon this capital. Fire came out of it, and my empire perishes by it in this place." Then came to him a messenger from his house, saying, "O Emperor of Rome, what causes thee to linger, when thy beloved son is dead?" And the Emperor of Rome spoke to the kings, and the troops, and the priests, and the thousands who could not be counted, and they went away with him till they came to his dwelling ; and his wife came out and said to him, "O Emperor of Rome, what is thy throne, when thy son, thy loved one, is dead? Come let us weep over our only (child) to-day."

And there came the daughter of the door-keeper, who had

been healed from the leprosy, and she entered to the Emperor of Rome, and said to him, "O Emperor of Rome, what makes thee <sub>page 13</sub> weep for thy only (child) as (thou dost) this day? There is in the city a weak old man, wearing rags. Seek him, and he will raise this only (child) of thine."

And the Emperor of Rome said to her, "O damsel, thou puttest me to shame. Shall the stones speak, or the blind see, or the dead rise? and how dost thou say that my only (child) shall rise? Come, weep for my only (child) this day, (thou) and all thy companions."

And she said to him, "O Emperor of Rome, dost thou know me?"

He said to her, "Yes, thou art the daughter of the door-keeper, the leprous one."

She said to him, "O Emperor of Rome, I am not leprous." And she uncovered her fore-arm and her face.

And when he looked at her, he said to her, "Ah, thou damsel, how is this that I see thee to-day?"

She said to him, "In truth I say to thee, O Emperor of Rome, <sub>page 14</sub> that the weak and poor old man whom I mentioned to thee, he it is who has cured me, and he will raise thy son and thy only (child) this day."

And he sent to all the kings and the priests, and said to them, "Seek for this old man of whom this girl speaks." And the kings and the priests sought for Peter, until they met him in the city in his rags. And they brought him in to the Emperor of Rome. And the Emperor of Rome said to him, "O old man, if thou wilt raise my son and my only (child) this day, then mine empire (shall be) thine." And Peter said to him, "Thy son and thy only (child) I will raise, but thine empire I do not want. Yet I want one word, that thou wilt serve my Lord and my God, Jesus <sub>page 15</sub> the Christ, Creator of Heaven and earth, besides whom there is no God, and that thou wilt leave these gods and idols whom thou servest."

And the Emperor of Rome said to him, "O Peter, this shall be thine if thou wilt raise my son."

And Peter said to the Emperor of Rome, "Send to thy kings, and to the troops, and to the priests among the people of thine empire, those who come in and go out, and assemble them, and carry this thy dead son upon his couch, and come to the place of thy god whom thou servest."

And the Emperor of Rome sent to all the kings and the priests and the captains, and he carried his only son on his couch. And he went to the place of the idols whom he had worshipped, and Peter stood alone by the side of the couch, calling on the Christ, page 16 and saying, "My Lord and my God, thou art He who hast sent me to Rome for the welfare and salvation of her people, and thou art He who hast caused the death of this sinner for the salvation of all by my resurrection of him in Thy name; therefore reveal at this time Thy power at my mention of Thy name, and the name of Thy Incarnation." And when he said this, the dead [man], the son of the king, arose from his bed, till he came to Peter; and he did him homage, and said,

"Peace unto thee, O disciple of the Christ,

Peace unto thee, O holy one of God,

Peace unto thee, who writest what the angels say to thee,

Peace unto thee, whose prayer the King has answered, so that my spirit has returned to my body."

Then the dead man who had risen turned to his father, the Emperor of Rome, and said,

page 17          "Woe unto thee, O my father, and what have we worshipped?

"Woe unto thee, O my father, and what sins are ours?

"Woe unto thee, O my father, for this old man calls thee to a great God and terrible in power, and the angels hold discourse with this old man!

"Woe unto thee, O my father, and in what darkness we are!

"Let the Emperor straightway believe in God this day; and all the kings and the priests."

And the Emperor said to his son, "Tell me thy story."

And the youth said to him, "When I was snatched away, I journeyed to the furthest end of Heaven, and when I went

before the Throne of Glory, this old man was standing there
doing homage, and the legions of Angels standing by. And the
Lord said from His throne, ' Let the desire of Peter, the captain
of My church, be fulfilled.' And at this voice my soul returned page 18
to my body."

And the Emperor said to Peter, " O Lord, command us as
thou wilt."

And Peter rose, and filled a font in the place where their gods
were, and baptized the Emperor and his son, and all his patriarchs,
and all the priests and the captains, till Peter was not able to
baptize the people from their number, till Peter took some of the
water of the font, and sprinkled (it) upon the people, and on
whomsoever one drop fell, he was baptized. And all the people
of Rome believed ; and Peter dwelt in it preaching, and baptizing,
and teaching, and the people came from every side, and were
baptized by him, and believed in the Christ, and forsook the world,
and renounced family and goods, and sought for faith in the page 19
Christ, to whom be glory now and for ever and ever, Amen.
And glory be continually to God. And upon us be mercy.
Amen.

# MARTYRDOM OF JAMES THE SON OF ALPHÆUS.

THIS is the Martyrdom of James the son of Alphæus, and the end of his warfare on the ninth day of October, in the peace of the Lord, Amen.

It was when James went into the city of Jerusalem to proclaim the holy Gospel in it, and all the wonders of the Godhead, that every one who heard him might believe in God with a pure heart and his soul might be saved. But James the Disciple thought in his heart how the crowd might hear him and believe in God, and that he would go into the temple where the crowd was assembled. And he found many of the Jews gathered together, and he began to preach in the midst of them, with great joy and gladness before their assembly. And he continued his speech, and explained (about) faith in God. And he testified concerning the only Son of God, the Word of life, God of all the ages, Jesus the Christ, that He is the Son of God in truth, and that He is the self-existent with the Father before all the ages. He is in the Father, and the Father is in Him, He who is the Word of the Father. Behold, He said, "Let us make man in our image and form;" and He dwelleth in Heaven with His Father, and He is upon the throne of the cherubim, and the seraphim extol Him. And He it is who is on the right hand of power on high. And He descended into the <sub>page 2</sub> womb of the Virgin Mary. And He is the Lord Jesus the Christ, to whom the Lady Mary the Virgin gave birth, and He is the God who was made man. This is the confession of the Disciple before that assembly, without fear of any other man.

He testified concerning the birth of the only Son of God, and he testified to His death and His resurrection from the dead, and His ascension to His Father who is in Heaven. And he taught faith in the Christ to all who were present. And when the assembly heard what the Disciple said, they were angry with a great anger, which (was) from their father the Devil, who dwelt in them, against the disciple of the Lord Jesus the Christ. And they helped one another, and took his blood upon them, all who were present and heard his discourse. And they seized the blessed Disciple, and led him to the Emperor Claudius, and set up against him false witnesses. And they said to the Emperor, "This man is a seducer. He goes round about countries and cities, and he says, 'I am the servant of Jesus the Christ.' And he hinders them from obeying the Emperor." And when the Emperor heard this about the blessed Disciple, he commanded him to be stoned with stones until he was dead. And the Jews (may God curse them!) stoned him as the Emperor had commanded. And such was the Martyrdom of the Disciple James the son of Alphæus, brother of Matthew, on the ninth day of the month of October. And he was buried beside the temple in Jerusalem. Glory be to God continually for ever.

# PREACHING OF SIMON SON OF CLEOPHAS.

THIS is the preaching of the blessed and holy Simon son of Cleophas, who was called Jude, which is, being interpreted, Nathanael, who was called the Zealot, and was bishop in Jerusalem after James the brother of the Lord Jesus the Christ.

It was when the disciples were gathered together on the Mount of Olives that they might divide all the cities of the world. And while they prayed and blessed God (may His Name be glorified!) the Lord Jesus the Christ was present in the midst of them, and said unto them, "May the peace of my Father rest upon you, O my pure disciples." And when they cast lots, the lot of Jude the Galilæan came out for the regions of Samaria, that he should preach in them the gospel of the Lord Jesus the Christ. And Simon answered and said unto the Lord, " Be with us, O our Lord, in every place where we dwell, and we will be patient in all that may happen to us. But let my father Peter go out with me, that he may bring me to the land of Samaria." And the Lord said unto him, " Peter's lot is that he should go out to Rome to preach there. But yet let him go out with thee, until he brings thee [there] in peace. And I say unto thee, that after thy preaching and thy calling to them, thou shalt return to Jerusalem after the death of James the Just, and thou shalt be bishop there after him. And thou shalt finish thy warfare like as James the Just (shall have) finished it in that place. And now, friend Simon, go out in peace. May the power of my Father go with thee." And page 2 the Lord blessed him, he and all the disciples, and He ascended to Heaven in great glory. And after the ascension of the Lord

to Heaven, Simon arose and prayed; and he went down to Jerusalem, and Peter with him, and they travelled to Samaria. And
he proclaimed in it the good news of the Gospel. And Simon
the disciple went into the midst of their synagogue, and proclaimed in it the name of Jesus the Christ. And when the Jews
who dwelt in that place heard it, they rose up against him,
and smote him with painful blows, and thrust him out
of the city. And Peter kissed him and took leave of him.
And Simon returned, and stood in their synagogue for three
days preaching among them the name of Jesus the Christ.
And some among them believed, and some did not believe
And in the last day, the third one, the son of the ruler of the
synagogue fell sick, and his name was James, and he died. And
one of the men who believed what Simon had said presented
himself to the father of the dead lad, and said unto him, " There is
here a disciple of the Christ. Call him to pray over the lad." And
the man went in haste, and called the Disciple of our Lord the
Christ and he came joyfully, and stood over the dead boy, and said
to the father of the boy who was dead, " Dost thou believe
in Him who was crucified, that He is the Son of God ? Thereupon thou shalt see the glory of God." The father of the
boy said unto him, " If my son should rise from the dead,
so that I see him alive, I will believe in Jesus the Crucified, that page 3
He is the Son of the living God." And the Disciple turned with
his face to the east, and prayed and said, " My Lord Jesus the
Christ, who wast crucified by command of Pilate the Pontius, thou
hast thought me worthy of this service, that I should preach in
Thy blessed name, because thou hast taken this body for our sake,
to save us from the hand of the enemy. Look upon this dead
boy, and by Thy will command him to rise, that Thy name may
be glorified this day in the midst of this whole city, that they
may believe in Thy holy name." And when Simon, the blessed
Disciple, said this, he turned towards the place where the dead
boy was, and said, " In the name of the Father, and of the Son,
and of the Holy Ghost, let him rise and stand up alive ! And be
thou whole, so that all who are present may believe in the name

of my Lord Jesus the Christ!" And in that hour the boy opened his eyes, and rose and sat up. And he commanded that they should offer him something to eat. And when the crowd saw this wonder, they all came forward and bowed down to the earth to the Disciple, and they all believed in God, and they were saying, "There is one God, and Simon is the Disciple of Jesus the Christ. We believe in Jesus the Christ, that He is the Son of the living God." And the parents of the boy threw themselves at the feet of the Disciple, and said, "O our Lord, how may we be saved?" He said unto them, "Believe with all your hearts, and ye shall be saved." And he exhorted them from the page 4 holy Scriptures, and he baptized them in the name of the Father, and of the Son, and of the Holy Ghost, and he gave them the holy mysteries, and commanded them to build a church, and appointed them a bishop, who was the ruler of the synagogue, and his name was Cornelius. And he appointed them presbyters and deacons, and he gave them the holy Gospel. And he stayed with them a month, teaching them the word of God. And after that he returned to Jerusalem. And when the Jews killed James, the disciples were gathered together in Jerusalem. They took Simon and made him bishop in Jerusalem. And he taught them the word of God, and made known to them what was in the Gospel, and the salvation of their souls. And the Jews were angry with him, and he was in Jerusalem giving praise to the Lord Jesus the Christ at all times and seasons, and may the same be to Him for ever and ever. Amen.

# MARTYRDOM OF SIMON.

THIS is the Martyrdom of Simon son of Cleophas, Disciple of the Lord Jesus the Christ. He finished his warfare on the eighth day of the month of May, at peace with the Lord. Amen.

It was after the mourning for James the Just, that Simon son of Cleophas, who was called Jude, became bishop of Jerusalem. And he lived a hundred and twenty years, and he said at the end of his life, "I wish that my blood may be shed for the name of the Lord Jesus the Christ." And he built churches in every place in Jerusalem. And he appointed them presbyters and deacons, and the first church which page 5 he built was in the name of the Lord Jesus the Christ; and the second in the name of the Virgin Mary, Mother of the Lord upon earth, of Him who turned the race of man from the worship of devils, and thought them worthy of His kingdom; and the third he called by the name of Michael, chief of the Angels, who is Mediator for the human race, that wrath may be turned away from them and mercy may rest upon them. And the fourth he called by the name of the Disciple; and he wished the faith of the Jews to be brought to nought, as well as their polluted worship and their wicked synagogue. And he sat preaching the Word of God to every-one, that he should frequent the churches which he had built, and that the knowledge of God might appear to all people from the greatest to the smallest, both men and women. And all of them believed by means of the Disciple, until the people of the city forsook the synagogue of the Jews, and followed the truth which the Disciple taught them by means of the Lord Jesus But as for the Jews, when they heard of the work of the blessed Disciple, and that he wished the destruction of their worship, and

A. P. 9

their exile, they all gathered together, great and small, and took counsel together concerning the Disciple to kill him as [he was] a worker of iniquity. And thus all the Jews assembled against him in anger and hate; and they put him in chains, and delivered him to the Emperor Hadrian. And they together bore witness against him before the Emperor, and said unto him, "Hear

page 6 us, we make known to thee what this magician does." And the Emperor was angry with a great anger at all that they said against the Disciple, and said unto him, "I say unto thee, O worker of iniquity, it has been told me that thou art a magician, and hast bewitched every one in this town." The Disciple said unto him, "Hear, from me, I pray, O Emperor, who hast neither understanding nor sense, I am not a magician, and I do not know how the art of magic is performed. But I am a servant of my Lord Jesus the Christ, God of all creation, and King of Kings, the powerful God, the Mighty, He who destroys all the gods of the heathen." And when the Emperor heard that speech from the Disciple, he was angry with a great anger, and delivered him to wicked people to crucify him. And the Jews were ravening against him, and they took out the blessed Disciple Simon son of Cleophas to crucify, as the godless Emperor had commanded. And they hanged him on a cross, and tortured him till he died. And he finished his martyrdom on the tenth day of the month of May, and to God the Almighty be glory and honour throughout all ages. Amen.

ܐܟܬܘܒܐ

ܡܢ ܦܠܘܛܐܣ

ܠܥܠ ܡܠܦܢܘܬܐ ܘܡܝܣ

# ANAPHORA PILATI.

Tischendorf
Ev. Apoc. r. a.
p. 435

5

Tisch. r. b.
p. 443

Tisch. r. a.
p. 436

10

[1] On the margin is added :

[2] Cod.

ܐܚܝܕ ܟܠ. ܕܒܫܡܝܐ ܘܒܐܪܥܐ ܩܕܡ ܡܠܟ ܪ̈ܗܘܡܝܐ. ܡܘܕܥ
ܐܢܐ ܕܒܝܗܘܕܐ ܡܕܝܢܬܐ ܕܒܡܕ̈ܢܚܐ ܡܫܬܪܝܬܐ[1] ܕܒܠܝܫܡ Tisch. r. b. p. 444
ܬ̈ܒܝܢܬܐ. ܐܘܪܫܠܡ. ܟܠܗ ܟܢܫܐ ܕܝܗ̈ܘܕܝܐ ܐܫܠܡܘ
ܠܝ ܓܒܪܐ ܚܕ ܕܝܫܘܥ ܕܡܬܩܪܐ ܗܘܐ ܫܡܗ. ܕܟܕ ܣܓܝܐܬܐ
ܗܘܘ ܒܐܝܕܗ ܚܠܠܬܐ ܘܬܕܡܪ̈ܬܐ ܐܝܠܝܢ ܕܒܫܘܡܠܝܐ ܗܘ̈ܝ.
ܘܠܐ ܕܝܢ ܡܫܬܡܥܝܢ ܗܘܘ ܕܢܫܡ̈ܥܘܢܝܗܝ ܒܟܗܢ̈ܐ. ܟܢܫܐ ܕܝܢ
ܐܪܟܘܣ ܟܠܗܘܢ ܡܫܡܥܝܢ ܗܘܘ ܒܨܪܐ ܠܟܠܗܘܢ. ܕܐܪ̈ܟܢ page 2
ܗܘܐ ܠܗܘܢ ܫܡܗ. ܕܠܘ ܡܕܡ ܐܝܬܘܗܝ ܒܥܠܬܐ ܘܠܐ
ܢܛܪܘܬܗ. ܐܬܘ̈ܬܐ ܕܝܢ ܘܬܕܡܪ̈ܬܐ ܣܓ̈ܝܐܬ ܗܘܐ ܒܗ
ܒܝܘܡܐ ܗܢܐ ܕܥܒܕܬܐ. ܟܕ ܗܘ ܡܫܪܝܢܐ ܥܒܕܢܐ. ܠܣܡ̈ܝܐ
ܓܪ̈ ܦܬܚ ܠܗܘܢ ܥܝܢ̈ܝܗܘܢ ܘܚܓܝ̈ܪܐ ܐܣܝ ܕܢܗܠܟܘܢ.
ܘܠܡܚܓ̈ܪܐ ܕܢܗܘܘܢ ܚ̈ܠܝܡܝܢ. ܘܠܡܝ̈ܬܐ ܐܩܝܡ.
ܘܠܡܪ̈ܥܐ ܐܣܝ ܘܐܗܒ ܠܗܘܢ ܚܘܠܡܢܐ: ܕܠܐ ܡܫܟܚܝܢ
ܡܬܢܓܕܝܢ ܗܘܘ ܦܓ̈ܪܝܗܘܢ. ܐܦ ܚܕ ܡܢ ܓܒܪ̈ܝܗܘܢ ܠܡܦܓܪܘ.
ܘܠܝܬ ܗܘܐ ܡܕܡ ܕܡܬܬܪܝܨ ܟܠ ܟܠܗ: ܐܠܐ ܐ ܢ ܘܠܐ
ܟܠܝܗܘܢ. ܘܠܗܠܝܢ ܝܗܒ ܠܗܘܢ ܚܝܠܐ ܕܢܗܘܘܢ ܡܗܠܟܝܢ Tisch. r. a. p. 437
ܘܪܗܛܝܢ. ܘܠܓܪ̈ܒܐ ܦܩܕ ܘܐܬܕܟܝܘ.. ܘܐܣܝܘܬܐ ܕܐܪܒܥܐ
ܡܢ ܟܠܗܘܢ: ܗܝ ܕܐܦ ܠܐ̈ܠܗܐ ܬܕܡܘܪܬܐ ܫܒܝܚܬܐ.
ܠܡܝܬܐ ܕܐܝܬ ܗܘܐ ܠܗ ܒܫܝܘܠ ܐܪ̈ܒܥܐ ܝܘ̈ܡܝܢ.
ܒܡܠܬܐ ܟܠܚܘܕ ܩܪܐ ܠܗ ܘܩܡ. ܐܝܟܐ ܕܐܝܬܘܗܝ
ܗܘܐ ܒܚܘܪܐ ܕܒܝܬ ܩܒܪܐ. ܘܦܩܕ ܗܘܐ ܠܗ ܦܓܪܗ
ܒܪܘܚܬܐ ܘܒܡܘܠܒܐ ܕܐܪܒܥܐ ܪܦܬ ܗܘܐ ܠܓܘܫܡܗ

[1] Cod. ܡܫܪ̈ܝܬܐ

Tisch. r. b.
p. 445

Tisch. r. a.
p. 438

Tisch. r. b.
p. 446

Tisch. r. a.
p. 439

ܪ̈ܘܪܒܢ ܡܢ ܗܠܝܢ ܚܕܐ ܗܘܐ ܗܘܐ ܝܫܘܥ. ܕܐܦ ܡܢ
ܐ̈ܠܗܐ ܕܦܓܪܢܝܢ ܠܗܘܢ: ܪ̈ܘܪܒܢ ܘܬܫ̈ܒܚܬܗܘܢ:

ܠܗ ܕܝܢ ܠܗܢܐ ܐܢ̈ܫܘܗܝ ܘܐܪ̈ܟܘܢܘܗܝ ܘܫܠܝ̈ܛܢܘܗܝ
ܘܢܟܣܝܢ ܘܡܥܒܕܐ. ܗ̣ܢܘܢ ܗܠܝܢ ܐܫܠܡܘܗܝ ܠܗ ܒܗܢ
ܗܓܡܘܢܐ ܕܝܗ̈ܘܕܝܐ. ܘܡܛܠܬܗ ܕܗܢܐ ܗܓܡܘܢܘܬܗ ܪܒܬܐ
ܐܡܝܢܐ ܥܠ ܟܠܢܫ ܕܐܪ̈ܩܝܡܘܗܝ. ܘܗܟܢ ܐܬܦܪܣܬ
ܕܐܦ̈ܝܣܘܗܝ ܘܠܐ ܐܫܟܚܬ. ܘܟܕ ܚܙܝܬ ܪܘܒܐ ܕܦܠܐܡ
ܥܠ ܡܛܠܬܗ: ܫܕܪܬ ܠܘܬܟܘܢ ܐܦܘܡܢܣܝܣ ܕܣܝܓܠܠ. page 3
ܡܢ ܡܕܡܐܡܬ ܢܓܕ ܠܗ ܗܘܝܬ ܒܦ̈ܓܠܐ. ܟܕ ܚܙܐ
ܥܠܬܐ ܕܚܫ̈ܝܒܐ ܠܗ ܠܡܚܬܐ ܠܐ ܐܫܟܚܬ ܠܗܬ
ܟܒܪܐ ܗܢܐ. ܡܢ ܥܠܡܝܢ ܡܐܠܓܘܪ̈ܝܘܗܝ ܕܡܬܠܝܢ ܗܘܘ
ܒܬܪܗ. ܘܟܕ ܐܣܓܠܠ ܗܘܐ ܗ̇ܘ ܗܢܐ ܝܫܘܥ ܥܠ ܩܝܣܐ
ܐܚܕ ܗܘܐ ܚܫܘܟܐ ܐܪܥܐ ܟܠ ܥܠܡܝܢ ܒܬ̈ܪܬܐ.
ܒܦܠܓܗ ܕܝܘܡܐ ܠܐ ܕܢܚ ܗܘܐ ܠܗ ܫܡܫܐ. ܘܢܘܗܪܗ Tisch. r. b. p. 447
ܕܣܗܪܐ ܐܝܟ ܕܡܐ ܡܬܚܙܐ ܗܘܐ. ܘܟܘܟܒܐ ܗܠܟܐ
ܕܝ̈ܗܘܕܝܐ ܐܬܟܠܒ ܒܐܪܥܐ. ܘܪ̈ܟܒܐ ܘܟܪ̈ܘܒܐ ܙ̈ܢܝܐ
ܗܘܘ. ܘܡܟܪ̈ܒܐ ܦ̈ܓܠܐ ܐܬܦܫܝܘ. ܘܡܫ̈ܝܚܬܐ ܦ̈ܓܠܐ Tisch. r. a. p. 440
ܡܢܗ ܡܢ ܡܟܪ̈ܝܗܘܢ. ܘܬܪ̈ܥܝܬܐ ܐܟܡܬܐ ܥܡ ܐܒܪܗܡ
ܘܐܝܣܚܩ ܘܝܥܩܘܒ ܗ̈ܠܝܢ ܕܢܦܩܘ ܗܘܘ ܡܢ ܥܠܡܐ. ܐܝܟ
ܕܡܢ ܡܕܡ ܬ̈ܪܝܢ ܫ̈ܠܝܢ ܕܩ̈ܒܝܪܐ. ܫܡܥܬ ܐܢܐ ܟܒ̈ܢܝ ܟܣܦܪ.
ܒܕ ܐܦ ܠܟܠ ܐܢܫ ܐܬܚܙܝܘ. ܘܩܥܝܢ ܗܘܘ ܘܒܟܝܢ ܡܬܢܐܪܐܬ:
ܡܛܠ ܒܥܠܐ ܪܐܒܐ ܕܗܘܐ. ܘܡܛܠ ܐܟܒܪܐ ܕܝ̈ܗܘܕܝܐ

Tisch. r. a.<br>p. 441

Tisch. r. b.<br>p. 448

<hr>

[1] The word is wanting in the MS.

 page 4

 Tisch r. a.
p. 442; r. b.
p. 449
[PARADOSIS PILATI]

ܕܐܣܬܒܪ ܡܢ ܦܝܠܛܘܣ. ܗܝܕܝܢ ܐܬܡܠܝ ܗܘܐ ܛܒܪܝܘܣ ܩܣܪ ܚܡܬܐ ܪܒܬܐ. ܘܦܩܕ ܗܘܐ ܪܘܟܒܗ ܥܠ ܦܝܠܛܘܣ. ܐܝܟ ܬܢܝܢܐ ܡܢ ܐܬܘܪܐ˙ ܘܒܪܘܓܙܐ ܕܫܡܥܬܗ ܦܩܕ ܗܘܐ ܪ̈ܗܛܐ ܕܢܐܬܘܢܝܘܗܝ ܡܢ ܐܘܪܫܠܡ ܠܪܘܡܝ ܒܝܕ ܪܗܛܐ ܪܒܐ. ܐܝܟ ܕܠܓܒܪܐ ܚܒܝܫ ܒܩ̈ܛܝܪܬܐ ܀ ܗܝܕܝܢ ܢܚܬܘ ܗܘܘ ܪ̈ܗܛܐ ܐܝܟ ܦܘܩܕܢܗ ܕܩܣܪ. ܘܐܚܕܘܗܝ

Tisch. p. 450 ܗܘܘ ܠܦܝܠܛܘܣ ܘܐܝܬܝܘܗܝ. ܒܫ̈ܫܠܬܐ ܕܦܪܙܠܐ܆ ܘܗܒܘܗܝ ܐܣܩܘܗܝ ܠܪܘܡܝ ܓܝܪ ܡܫܐܪܝܘܣ ܀ ܗܝܕܝܢ ܟܕ ܫܡܥ ܗܘܐ ܩܝܣܪܐ ܛܒܪܝܘܣ ܕܥܠ ܦܝܠܛܘܣ ܠܪܘܡܝ. ܦܩܕ ܕܢܬܟܢܫܘܢ ܠܗ ܒܟܢܘܫܬܐ. ܟܠܗ ܡܢ ܢܘ̈ܩܐ ܕܐ̈ܠܗܐ ܕܫ̈ܪܟܐ. ܟܕ ܝܬܒܐ ܗܘܬ ܒܗܢܗ ܟܠܗ̇ ܣܘܢܩܠܝܛܘܣ ܕܠܗ. ܘܟܠܗܘܢ ܐܝܠܝܢ ܕܐܚܝܕܝܢ ܗܘܘ ܕܪ̈ܓܐ ܕܣܘ̈ܢܩܠܝܛܐ. ܘܟܕ ܟܢܝܫܝܢ ܗܘܘ ܟܠܗܘܢ ܚܝ̈ܠܘܬܐ ܕܣܢܩܠܝܛܘܣ܆ ܥܠ ܗܘܐ ܘܝܬܒ ܒܝܘܡܐ ܥܠ ܒܝܡ ܀ ܗܝܕܝܢ ܦܩܕ ܗܘܐ ܕܢܩܪܒܘܢܝܘܗܝ ܠܗ ܠܦܝܠܛܘܣ ܩܕܡ ܒܝܡ ܕܕܝܢܐ. ܘܟܕ ܥܠ ܗܘܐ ܦܝܠܛܘܣ ܘܩܡ ܩܕܡܘܗܝ. ܒܥܐ ܛܒܪܝܘܣ ܘܐܡܪ ܠܗ. ܡܛܠ ܐܝܢܐ ܗܠܝܢ ܕܥܒܕܬ ܒܗ̇ ܒܪܫܝܥܘܬܟ. ܬ̈ܕܡܪܬܐ ܕܐܝܟ ܗܠܝܢ ܐܬܚܙܝ ܠܟ: ܘܠܓܒܪܐ ܗܘ̇ ܒܝܫܐܝܬ ܐܡܪܚܬ ܕܬܨܠܒܝܘܗܝ: ܘܥܠܡܐ ܟܠܗ ܡܢ ܐܘܟܡܢ ܐܠܒܫܬ ܚܫܘܟܐ ܀ ܗܝܕܝܢ ܒܥܐ ܗܘܐ ܦܝܠܛܘܣ ܘܐܡܪ ܠܗ. ܦܐܘܛܘܩܪܛܘܪ. ܐܢܐ ܕܕܠܐ ܥܠܬܐ ܒܥܠܬܐ ܐܝܬܝ ܒܗܕܐ. ܐܝܠܝܢ ܕܒܫܠܘܬܐ ܗܕܐ ܐܬܥܒܕܘ: ܗܘܠܓܐ ܕܝܗ̈ܘܕܝܐ ܐܝܬܝܗܘܢ. ܘܒܥܐ ܗܘܐ ܩܣܪܝܘܣ

ܘܐܡܪ ܠܗ. ܘܡܢ ܐܢܘܢ ܗܠܝܢ. ܐܡܪ ܠܗ ܦܝܠܐܛܘܣ.
ܐܝܪܘܕܝܣ ܕܡܬܩܪܐ ܐܪܟܠܐܘܣ ܘܦܝܠܝܦܘܣ. ܘܚܢܐܢ
ܘܩܝܦܐ. ܘܟܠܗ ܣܘܓܐܐ ܕܝܗ̈ܘܕܝܐ ܀ ܗܘ ܕܝܢ ܡ̈ܠܟܐ
ܦܩܕ ܠܗ ܦܬܓܡܐ ܘܐܡܪ. ܡܛܠ ܐܢܫܐ ܛܒܝܐ ܕܟܢܫܬ
ܐܢܘܢ ܘܫܠܡܬ ܠܗܘܢ ܘܐܫܬܠܡܬ ܠܡܫܠܡܢܘܬܗܘܢ. ܒܢܝܐ
ܦܝܠܐܛܘܣ ܘܐܡܪ ܠܗ. ܐܢܫܐ ܒܢ̈ܝ ܐܘܪܫܠܡ ܘܕܠܐ
ܫܘܥܒܕܐ ܐܝܬܘܗܝ. ܟܠܗ ܥܡܐ ܕܝܠܗܘܢ. ܘܠܐ
ܡܫܬܥܒܕܝܢ ܗܢܘ ܠܫܘܠܛܢܐ ܪܒܐ ܕܐܘܓܣܛܘܣ ܀ ܗܝܕܝܢ page 5
ܒܝܫܐ ܗܘܐ ܣܛܪ ܘܐܡܪ ܠܗ. ܘܟܕ ܐܫܬܠܡܘܗܝ ܗܘܘ
ܠܝ. ܡܬܬܒܥܝܢ ܗܘܐ ܕܬܫܬܥܒܕܘܢ ܘܬܬܕܒܪܘܢ ܒܗ : ܘܟܕ Tisch. p. 451
ܐܢܫܐ ܡܢ ܩ̈ܠܝܣܐ ܕܡ̈ܠܟܘܬܝ : ܬܫܬܕܪܘܢ ܠܘܬܝ
ܒܗܝܪܘܬܐ ܪܒܬܐ: ܘܠܐ ܬܬܦܩܘܢ ܠܡܫܠܡܢܘܬܗܘܢ ܕܝܗ̈ܘܕܝܐ
ܬܬܓܠܒܘܢ. ܠܓܒܪܐ ܕܐܝܬܘܗܝ ܗܘܐ ܙܕܝܩܐ. ܘܕܗܠܝܢ
ܗܘܒܪ̈ܐ ܥܒ̈ܕܐ ܗܒܪ ܠܗ. ܒܪ ܐܢܫ ܐܫܬܘܕܝܬ
ܘܐܡܪܬ ܒܝܕ ܐܢܦܘܪܐ ܡܘܕܒܢܘܬܐ ܕܡܫܝܚ ܐܬܩܪܝܬ
ܠܝ ܒܪ ܐܠܗ ܗܘܐ ܕܢܬܓܠܒ. ܕܗܢܐ ܡܫܝܚܐ ܡ̈ܠܟܐ
ܕܝܗ̈ܘܕܝܐ ܀ ܘܟܕ ܗ̈ܠܝܢ ܐܡܪ ܗܘܐ. ܘܐܬܕܒܪ
ܗܘܐ ܫܡܗ ܕܡܫܝܚܐ. ܟܠܗܘܢ ܨ̈ܠܡܐ ܕܐܝܬ ܗܘܐ[1]
ܒܢܘܣܐ ܗܘ ܢܦܠܘ ܘܐܬܬܒܪܘ. ܘܗܘܝܐ ܐܫܬܒܩܘ ܐܝܟ
ܒܘܪܐ. ܒܢܫܐ ܕܝܢ ܟܠܗ ܕܩܝܡܝܢ ܗܘܘ ܬܡܢ ܩܕܡ ܩܣܪ.
ܒܙܝܥܘܬܐ ܪܒܬܐ ܘܒܐܪܬܘܬܐ ܗܘܘ ܠܗܘܢ. ܡܛܠ
ܡܦܠܬܐ ܕܨ̈ܠܡܐ. ܘܡܛܠ ܡ̈ܠܐ ܕܡܠܟܐ ܕܐܬܐܡܪ̈ܝ.

[1] Sic in Cod.

---

¹ Cod. 

² The words  are added on the margin.

³ Cod. 

Tisch. p. 452

    page 6

    Tisch. p. 453

¹ Sic in Cod.

[Syriac text, 21 lines]

Tisch. p. 454

5

10

15

20

---

[1] Sic in Cod.    [2] Cod. [Syriac]    [3] Cod. [Syriac]

ܛܘܒܢܐ ܟܕ ܐܙܠ ܗܘܐ ܘܡܨܠܐ ܠܕܘܟܬܐ ܕܒܗ̇ ܒܬܪ. ܗܘܐ ܕܢܬܒܠܠ[1] ܡܢ ܡܪܗ: ܐܬܦܢܝ ܗܘܐ ܠܩܘܣܛܘܢܪܐ ܟܕ ܐܡܪ. ܡܦܝܣ ܐܢܐ ܠܟ ܐܚܝ ܡܛܠ ܫܘܒܚܗ ܕܡܪܢ ܝܫܘܥ ܡܫܝܚܐ. ܕܐܬܓܪ ܥܠ ܩܠܠ ܕܐܝܟܢܐ ܘܐܬܕܒܫ ܠܗܘ̇ ܕܗܒܐ ܡܛܠܬܗ ܡܢܟܠ ܐܢܐ ܡܫܩܡ ܒܥܝܐ ܗܘܢܐ ܕܡܘܬܐ ܒܝܕ ܫܘܒܐ ܗܘܢܐ ܚܪܝܦܐ. ܘܟܕ ܗܕ̈ܝܢ ܗܠܝܢ ܐܡܪ ܗܘܐ ܦܝܠܛܘܣ. ܐܬܦܝܣ ܠܗ ܠܡܘܒܠ ܡܕܢܚܐ. ܘܫܐܠ ܒܥܘ̈ܪܐ ܘܒܝܕ ܡܪܗ ܘܒܪ ܗܘܐ ܕܢܦܩ ܠܡܪܗ page 7 ܝܫܘܥ ܡܫܝܚܐ. ܒܟܐܒܐ ܡܪܝܪܢ ܐܠܗܐ ܕܟܠ ܠܟ ܡܪܢ ܝܫܘܥ ܡܫܝܚܐ ܕܐܬܐ ܠܦܘܪܩܢ ܘܟܠ ܡܪܝ ܒܥܘܬܗ ܕܥܒܕܝܢ ܒܥܒܕܐ ܗܘܝܐ. ܘܫܪܝ ܡܪܝ ܘܫܒܘܩ ܠܝ ܟܠ ܕܣܪܚܬ ܘܣܟܠܬ ܘܒܕܡܝܢ ܠܐ ܝܕܥ ܗܘܝܬ ܡܢܐ ܥܒܕ ܗܘܝܬ. ܘܠܐ ܡܪܝ ܬܫܒܘܩܝܗ̇ ܠܝ ܚܛܝܬܐ ܘܬܬܒܥܝܢ ܡܢ ܒܒܐ ܦܘܪܐ ܕܒܘܕܝܐ. ܡܛܠ ܕܐܢܐ ܠܐ ܝܕܥܐ ܗܘܝܬ ܕܐܦܫܪ ܒܕܡܝܢ ܫܦܝܪܐ ܐܢ̈ܫܝ. ܘܟܠ ܗܝ ܠܗ ܗܕܐ ܫܒܘܩ ܗܘܝܬ ܡܪ̈ܝܐ ܘܐܬܒܩܝܬ ܐܢ̈ܫܝ. ܘܐܬܦܪܩܬ ܕܐܢܐ ܡܫܝܚܐ ܐܒܐ ܗܘ ܕܡܢܗ ܕܗܘܢܐ ܕܝܘܕܝܐ. ܘܟܕ ܗܕܐ ܫܡܥܬ ܗܘܝܬ. ܗܕܝܢ ܡܢ ܗܘܐ ܥܠ ܒܐܘܓܣܛܘܣ ܩܣܪܐ ܚܪܒܐ ܕܝܘܕܝܐ. ܘܐܢܬ ܡܪܝ ܝܕܥ ܐܢܬ ܕܡܢ ܕܫܠܛܬܗ ܕܩܪܝ ܐܫܬܒܩܬܢ ܗܘܝܬ ܒܐܝܕܝܗܘܢ. ܘܐܢܬ ܡܪܝ ܘܐܠܗܝ ܝܕܥ ܗܘܝܬ. ܕܐܝܟ ܠܐ ܢܓܪ ܐܢܐ: ܡܢܐ ܥܒܕ ܐܢܐ ܥܒܕܬ ܗܕܐ. ܠܐ ܡܪܝ ܬܫܒܘܩ ܠܝ ܚܛܝܬܐ ܗܕܐ.

[1] Cod. ܕܢܬܒܠ

ܘܬܘܟܒܝܢ. ܐܠܐ ܐܬܕܒܪܝܢ ܠܗ ܘܠܐܬܩܢܟ ܦܪܘܩܠܐ.
ܠܗܕܐ ܕܘܡܝܐ ܚܡܝ ܒܐܓܘܢܐ ܟܕܘܢܐ ܗܢܐ. ܘܟܫܒܬܐ
ܗܕܐ ܡܫܪܬܐ ܕܟܫܘܬܐ. ܗܕܐ ܕܐܝܬ ܒܒܝܫܘܬܐ
ܒܗ ܐܬܚܙܝܬ ܕܬܓܠܓܠ ܠܐ ܬܬܕܟܪ ܠܗ ܡܪܝ. ܣܓܝܐܬܐ ܗܕܐ
Tisch. p. 455 ܘܬܬܒܟܫ ܒܐܘܪܚܝ: ܐܠܐ ܫܪܝ ܘܫܒܘܩ ܠܝ ܣܩܘܒܝܢ
ܘܣܦܩܝܢ. ܘܒܓܠܒܐ ܕܕܘܩܐ ܐܘܚܕܝܢ ܘܚܕܡܘ ܠܬܠܡܝܕܐ
ܒܡܠܘܬܟ. ܘܟܕ ܫܠܡ ܗܘܐ ܦܝܠܐܛܘܣ ܨܠܘܬܗ. ܗܐ
ܘܠܐ ܐܬܐ ܠܘܬܗ ܡܢ ܫܡܝܐ ܕܐܡܪ ܢܗܘܐ ܠܟ ܛܘܒܐ
ܒܢ̈ܝܐ ܕܥܠ ܐܪܥܐ. ܘܥܠܝܗܘܢ ܫܪܒܬܐ ܕܒܢ̈ܝܐ. ܡܛܠ
ܕܒܣܡܬܟ ܘܒܐܬܪܝܟ ܦܠܛ ܘܐܫܬܟܠܠ ܠܥܠܡ ܕܥܬܝܕ
ܒܢ̈ܒܝܐ ܡܬܠܠܬܝ. ܘܐܢܬ ܗܟܝܠ. ܬܗܘܐ ܠܗ ܫܪܝܐ
ܒܗܘ ܡܐܬܘܬܐ ܕܥܠܝ ܕܬܪܬܝܢ. ܡܟܐ ܕܐܬܐ ܐܢܫܐ
ܐܕܘ ܠܬܪܬܥܣܪܐ ܫܪܒܬܐ ܕܐܝܣܪܝܠ. ܘܠܐܠܦܝܢ ܕܠܐ
ܐܘܕܝܘ ܒܗ ܘܗܝܡܢܘ ܒܫܡܗ ܡܫܝܚܐ. ܘܟܕ ܕܝܢ ܗܢܐ
ܘܠܐ ܐܬܐ ܠܘܬܗ ܘܐܬܡܚܠܠ[1] ܒܚܘܒܗ. ܒܪܝܟ ܗܘܐ
ܘܣܐܡ ܒܘܪܟܐ ܥܠ ܐܪܥܐ ܘܐܡܪ ܠܣܦܩܘܠܛܪܐ. ܗܫܐ
ܩܪܘܒ ܘܫܩܘܠ ܡܢܗ ܕܐܬܦܩܕ ܠܟ ܡܢ ܡܪܝ. ܘܟܕ ܩܪܒ
ܣܦܩܘܠܛܪܐ ܘܢܣܒܗ ܒܣܝܦܐ ܘܩܛܠ ܪܝܫܗ ܕܦܝܠܐܛܘܣ.
ܗܝܕܝܢ ܢܚܬ ܗܘܐ ܡܠܐܟܐ ܕܐܠܗܐ ܡܢ ܫܡܝܐ. ܘܗܘ
ܩܒܠ ܪܝܫܗ ܕܦܝܠܐܛܘܣ. ܦܪܘܩܠܐ ܕܝܢ ܐܢܬܬܗ ܡܢܗܪܐ
ܗܘܬ ܘܚܙܬܐ ܒܗ. ܘܟܕ ܚܙܬ ܗܘܬ ܕܝܢ ܠܡܠܐܟܐ
ܕܐܠܗܐ ܕܩܒܠ ܠܪܝܫܗ ܕܒܥܠܗ. ܗܝܕܝܢ ܐܬܡܠܝܬ ܚܕܘܬܐ

[1] Cod. ܐܬܡܚܠܠܘ

ܪܒܬܐ. ܘܒܚܘܪܬܐ ܕܠܒܗ. ܐܫܠܡܬ ܢܦܫܗ ܠܡܪܗ. ܘܐܬܩܒܪܬ ܗܘܬ ܥܡ ܒܥܠܗ. ܘܫܒܩܘ ܗܘܘ ܐܢܛܘܢܝܘܣ ܒܣܗܕܘܬܐ ܦܠܛܬܐ. ܘܐܫܬܘܕܝܘ ܗܘܘ ܠܦܪܢܣܐ ܕܐܠܗܐ. ܘܡܨܝܚܝܢ ܗܘܘ ܫܦܝܪܐ ܕܡܬܘܕܝܢ ܘܐܬܒܢܝܘ. ܬܠܬܝܗܘܢ ܫܘܪܐ ܬܫܒܘܚܬܐ ܠܗ ܐܡܝܢ ܘܐܡܝܢ.

Then follows in the MS. the apocryphal correspondence of Herod and Pilate, which has already been published by Dr Wright in 'Contributions to the Apocryphal Literature of the New Testament.' Williams and Norgate, 1865.

ANAPHORA PILATI.   From No. 508.

*(From a photograph by A. S. Lewis.)*

To face first page of Arabic

تذكرة ما فعل بربنا يسوع المسيح على عهد بلاطس البنطى

من نسختان قديمتان موجودتان فى دير طور سينا

الاولى منهن مكتوبة فى سنة ١٨٣ من سنين العرب

الاخرى فى سنة لا نعرفها

# ANAPHORA PILATI. A.

هذه تذكرة ما فعل بربنا يسوع المسيح على عهد بيلاطس
البنطى والى اليهود فى سنة ثمانية عشر من ملك طباريوس القيصر
ملك الروم فى تسعة عشر سنة من بداة ملك هيرودس بن هيرودس

page 2 ملك اليهود فى خمسة وعشرين يوما خلت من ادار فى ولاية روفوا

5 وفى سنة اربعة من ولايتهم على عهد يوسيوس بن قيافاريس كهنة
اليهود وكل ما كان بعد الصليب ومصايب الرب وفعال روس الكهنة
وساير ذلك من اليهود جميع ما ابصر نقوديمس كتبه بالعبرانية

Tischen-
dorf, *Ev.*
*Apoc.* r. a.
P. 435 فى تلك الايام صلب ايسوع بامر بيلاطس فى ولايته على
فلسطين والساحل وهذه التذكرة فعلت فى بيت المقدس من اليهود

10 بالمسيح ورفعت الى طباريوس القيصر فى رومية قصة رفعها

page 3 بيلاطس بسبب ربنا والاهنا يسوع المسيح الى طباريوس القيصر برومية
فى تلك الايام عند ما صلب ربنا يسوع المسيح بامر بيلاطس البنطى
المتروس بفلسطين والساحل كانت هذه التذكرة بما فعلوا اليهود

Tisch. r. b.
P. 443 بالرب ان بيلاطس رفع الى قيصر برومية كتاب فيه هكذا الى القوى

15 المكرم المهاب طباريوس القيصر من بيلاطس من المشرق اتعاطيت

# ANAPHORA PILATI. B.

بسم الاب والابن وروح القدس اله واحد هذه تذكرة ما فعل
بسيدنا يسوع المسيح على عهد بلاطس البنطى والى اليهود فى
سنة ثمانية عشر من ملك طباريوس قيصر ملك الروم ∴ فى تسعة
اعشر سنة من ابتدا ملك هرودس ملك اليهود فى خمسة وعشرين
5 يوما خلت من ادار ∴ فى ولاية روفوا وروبيلينوس فى سنة اربعة
من ولايتهما ∴ على عهد يوسيوس بن قيافاريس كهنة اليهود وكلما
كان بعد الصلب واوجاع الرب وفعال ريسا الكهنة وساير ذلك من
اليهود وكلما ابصر نقودمس صيره فى كتب عبرانية ∴

page 2
Tischen-
dorf, *Ev.*
*Apoc.* r. a.
P. 435
فى تلك الايام صلب يسوع بامر بلاطس البنطى وولايته على
10 فلسطين والساحل وهذه التذكرة فعلت فى بيت المقدس من اليهود
بالمسيح ورفعت الى طباريوس قيصر فى رومية ∴ قصة رفعها
بلاطس من اجل ربنا والاهنا يسوع المسيح الى طباريوس برومية ∴
فى تلك الايام عند ما صلب ربنا يسوع المسيح بامر بلاطس البنطى
المتروس بفلسطين والساحل كانت هذه التذكرة بما فعلوه اليهود

Tisch. r. b.
P. 443
15 بالرب ∴ ان بلاطس رفع الى قيصر برومية كتاب فيه هكذا الى القوى
المكرم المهاب طباريوس قيصر ∴ من بلاطس من المشرق اتعاطيت

A. P.

3

Tisch. r. a.
p. 436
r. b. p. 444

ان اخبرك وانا مرتعد ايه القوى ان فى هذه البلدة التى ادبرها فى

بعض مدنها مدينة يقال لها اورشليم فيها جماعات لليهود وهم

page 4 اسلموا الي رجلا يقال له يسوع قايلين عليه ذنوب كثيرة وما لم يقدروا

ان يثبتوها عليه وبعض ما كانوا يوجبوه عليه انه كان يبطل حفظ

السبت وكان يفعل شفاء كثير واعمال صالحة وذلك انه كان يصير ٥

العمى يبصرون والمقعدين يمشون وموتى اقام ومخلعين ابرا الذين

لم يكن لهم اصلا قوة جسد ولا عروق ثابتة الا صوت ومفاصل فقط

Tisch. r. a.
p. 437 فوهب لهم قوة ان يمشون ويجرون وبكلمة واحدة كان يشفى

الامراض فالذى هو اقوى من هذا واعجب انه اقام ميت له اربعة ايام

فى القبر دعاه من الموتى وقد نتن من القيح والدود فى القبر فامره ان ١٠

page 5
Tisch. r. b.
p. 445 يجرى فجرى وليس فيه شى من اثارات الموت ولكن كمثل ختن من

حجلتة هكذا اُخرج من القبر ممتلى روح طيب وبالحقيقة *¹ مخابين

كان مساكنهم فى البرارى وياكلون لحومهم ويترددون مع السباع

والدبابات صيرهم اعفا وعقلا وحكما والارواح النجسة التى كانت

Tisch. r. a.
p. 438 تقاتلهم وهى فيهم مهلكة لهم رمى بها الى عمق البحر وايضا رجل ١٥

اخر كانت يده يابسة ونصف جسده ايضا كان قد يبس بكلمته اشفاه

وخلاه صحيحا وامراة ايضا تنزف الدم وقد انحلت عروقها ومفاصلها

من نزف الدم حتى انها ليس كانت تحمل جسد انسى بل

page 6 كانت تشبه الموتى الذين ليس لهم صوت فلم يكن استطاع احد

20 من الاطبا الذين فى البلدان يشفوها لانه لم يكون¹ بقى فيها رجا

Tisch. r. b.
p. 446 حياة فتحرّت ويسوع جايز اخذت قوة وبين الخلق امسكت بطرف

Tisch. r. a.
p. 439 ثوبه ومن ساعتها انقوت وبريت وبدت تجرى الى مدينتها بانياس

من كفرنحوم وكان ذلك منها غير قريب مسيرة ستة ايام وايضا رجل

اخر ولد اعمى من بطن امه ولم يكن له عينين اصلا فبزق على

---

¹ Sic in Cod.     * See note.

Tisch. r. a.<br>p. 436<br>r. b. p. 444

ان اخبرك وانا مرتعد ايه القوى لان فى هذا البلد الذى ادبره فى

بعض مدنه مدينة يقال لها اورشليم فيها خلق من اليهود وانهم

اسلموا الي رجلا يقال له يسوع قايلين عليه ذنوب كثيرة ما لم يقدروا

يثبتوها عليه وبعض ما كانوا يوجبوه عليه انه كان يبطل حفظ السبت

5 وكان يفعل ١ شفا كثير واعمال صالحة وذلك انه كان يصير العمى

يبصرون : والمقعدين يمشون واقام موتى ∴ ومخلعين ابرا الذين لم

٢يكون لهم اصلا قوة جسد ولا عروق ثابتة الا صوت فقط ومفاصل ∴

page 3<br>Tisch. r. a.<br>p. 437

فوهب لهم قوة يمشون ويجرون· وبكلمة فقط كان يشفى الامراض·

والذى هو اقوى من هذا واعجب انه احيا ميت له اربعة ايام نادى

10 به من الموتى وقد نتر من القيح والدود: موضوع فى القبر فامره

ان يجرى وليس فيه شى من اثارات الموت· لكن كمثل ختن من

Tisch. r. b.<br>p. 445

حجلته كذلك خرج من القبر ٢مملوا روح طيب وبالحقيقة ٭٢مخابين

كان ماواهم فى البرارى وياكلون لحومهم· ويترددون مع السباع

والدبابات صيرهم اعفا وحكما وعقلا والارواح النجسة التى تقاتلهم

Tisch. r. a.<br>p. 438

15 وهى فيهم مهلكة لهم رمى بهم الى غمق البحر وايضا رجل اخر

كانت يده يابسة ونصف بدنه ايضا يابس بكلمته اشفاه واصرفه

صحيحا ∴ ومرة ايضا كانت تنزف الدم عدة سنين حتى ان عروقها

ومفاصلها انحللت من نزيف الدم حتى انها ليس كانت تحمل

جسد انسى بل كانت تشبه الموتى ٢الذى ليس لهم صوت وما قدر

20 احد من الاطبا الذين فى البلدان على بروها لان ما كان بقى

Tisch. r. b.<br>p. 446

فيها رجا حياة منها ويسوع جايز اخذت قوة وامسكت بطرف ثوبه

Tisch. r. a.<br>p. 439

بين الخلق ومن ساعتها انقوت وبرت وذهبت تجرى الى مدينتها

بانيا من ٣كفرنحوم· وكان ذلك منها مسيرة ستة ايام· وايضا رجل

اخر ولد اعمى من بطن امه· لم ٢يكون عينين اصلا فبسق على

---

¹ Cod. سفا      ² Sic in Cod.      ³ Cod. كفرتنحوم.      * See note.

الارض وجعل طين ولطخ موضع عينيه وخلق له عينين يبصر بهما

وارسله الى مـا سلوان يغتسل به وفى السبت كـان ايسوع يعمل

اعاجيب افضل من هذه حتى بانى قد فهمت مـن عجايبه

اكثر ما فعلت الهتنا التى نعبدها فلهذا هيرودس وارشلاوس وفيلبس

وانيس وقيافا مع جميع الشعب اسلموه الي لكيما يهلكوه فعند

ما حركوا علي الشعب شغب كثير امرت ان يصلب بعد ان

ضربته بـالسياط ولـم اصب عليه علة فعال سوًا فلها صلب صارت

ظلمـة على الدنيا كلها واظلمت الشمس نصف النهار والكواكب

لم تظهر شعاعها والقمر انكشف وصار ضوه مثل الدم وكذلك ستر

هيكل اليهود انشق ومن شدة الزلزلة انشققت الصخور وظهروا الموتى

فى ذلك الفزع وقاموا كما شهدوا اليهود انهر نظروا الى ابرهيم واسحق

ويعقوب الابا وموسى وايوب الذين ماتوا كما قالوا اوليك من الفين

سنة وخمس ماية سنة وانا ايضا راينا كثيرين ظهروا فى الاجساد

وناحوا نوحا كثير لما صنع بيسوع من الفعل ¹القطيع وهلاك امة

اليهود وناموسهم ولم يهدا الخوف من ستة ساعات يوم الجمعة

الى عشية السبت وعشية سبت صباح الاحد صرخ صوت من السما

واضت السما اكثر من كل الايام سبعة اضعاف فى ثلثة ساعات

من الليل وظهرت الشمس مضية فى كل السما وكمثل برق الشتا

كذلك ظهروا رجال عظما بلباس بهى وتسبحة عظيمة وهم كثير لا

تحصوا صالحين وكانت اصواتهم عاليات مثل الرعد العظيم الاله

الذى صلب قد قام اصعد وامر الجحيم يا ايه المستعبدين فى

اسفل الارض وانشقت الارض حتى انه لـم يكن لها ثبات وهكذا

ظهرت ¹امياه الغمق مع صياح الذين كانوا فى السما وكانوا الموتى

page 7

Tisch. r. b.
p. 447

page 8
Tisch. r. a.
p. 440

page 9

Tisch. r. a.
p. 441

Tisch. r. b.
p. 448

¹ Sic in Cod.

الارض وصير طين ولطخ موضع عينيه وخلق له عينين يبصر بهما
وهذا الذى ذكرته جديدا فى عقلى اخبرت به وفى السبت كان
يعمل يسوع اعاجيب افضل من هذه حتى انى قد فهمت من

page 4

عجايبه اكثر مما فعلت الهتنا التى نعبدها ٠:٠ لهذا ¹هرودس وارشيلاوس
5	وفلبس وانس وقيافا مع جميع الشعب. شعب كثير اسلموه الي لكيما
يهلكوه ٠:٠ فلما حركوا علي الشعب شعب كثير امرت ان يصلب
بعد ما ضربته بالسياط ولم اجد عليه علة فعل ²سوا ٠:٠ فلما صلب
صارت ظلمة على الدنيا كلها واظلمت الشمس نصف النهار والكواكب

Tisch. r. b.<br>p. 447

لم تظهر شعاعا والقمر انكسف وصار نوره مثل الدم وكذلك ستر

Tisch. r. a.<br>p. 440

10	هيكل اليهود انشق ومن شدة الزلزلة تشققت الصخور وظهروا فى ذلك
الفزع الموتى وقاموا كما شهدوا اليهود انهم نظروا الى ابرهيم واسحق
ويعقوب الابا وموسى وايوب ²الذى ماتوا كما قالوا هوليك من الفين
سنة وخمسمايه سنة ٠:٠ وانا ايضا راينا كثيرين ظهروا فى الاجساد
وناحوا نوح كثير لما صنع بيسوع من الفعل القضيع ٠:٠ وهلاك امة

15	اليهود وناموسهم ٠:٠ ولم يهدا الخوف من ستة ساعات يوم الجمعة
الى عشية السبت وعشية يوم ³السبت صباح الاحد صرخ صوت من
السما واضت السما اكثر من كل الايام سبعة اضعاف ثلثة ساعات
من الليل وظهرت الشمس مضية فى كل السما وكمثل برق الشتا

Tisch. r. a.<br>p. 441

كذلك ظهروا رجال عظما بلباس بهى وتسبحة عظيمة وهم كثرة لا
20	يحصون صايحين وكانت اصواتهم عالية مثل الرعد العظيم قايلين
الاله الذى صلب قد قام اصعد وامر الجحيم يا بها المستعبدين

Tisch. r. b.<br>p. 448

فى اسافل الارض وانشقت الارض حتى ²يكون لها ثبات وكذلك
ظهرت ²امياه العمق مع صراخ ²الذى كانوا فى السما ٠:٠ وكانوا الموتى

---

¹ Cod. هروس	² Sic in Cod.
³ Cod. الشبت

الذين قاموا كثيرة كثيرة يمشون وانه سلب الجحيم موتاه وظهر

للنسوة وقال ¹لهم ¹قولوا للتلاميذ ان يتقدمونى الى الجليل

page 10 لانهم ثمة سايرونى وكل تلك الليلة لم يزل الضو ظاهرا

وكثيرين من اليهود ماتوا فى هوتة تلك الارض وابتلعوا حتى ان

٥ كثيرين لم يجدوا للغد ممن فعل بيسوع ما فعل وان مجامع

Tisch. r. a. p. 442 r. b. p. 449 اليهود فى اورشليم فروا ولم يظهر منهم احدا فلما رايت هذه الاشيا

المفزعة وبهتت نفسى رفعت الى قوتك وفسرت لك جميع ما فعلوا

Paradosis Pilati اليهود بيسوع وبعثت الى ملكك ⊕ ولما وصلت هذه الرسالة الى

القيصر وقريت بحضرة الناس كلهم صاروا مبهوتين عند ما سمعوا

page 11 ١٠ بخطيه بيلاطس كانت الزلزلة والظلمة على جميع المسكونة وان

القيصر امتلا غضبا وبعث فرسان لياتوا بيلاطس فى وثاق فلما

Tisch. p. 450 اتوا به الى مدينة رومية وسمع قيصر بان بيلاطس قد قدم قعد

فى موضع قوته وامر ان يقدم بيلاطس ويوقف قدامه فلما اوقفوه

قدامه قال له قيصر لماذا استجريت على مثل هذه الامور الكافرة

١٥ وانت قد رايت فى هذا الرجل هذه العلامات الشريفة ثم استجريت

على هذا الفعل السو واهلكت كل العالم وان بيلاطس اجاب قايل

page 12 يا القيصر ضابط الكل انا برى من هذا كله وانما علة هذا ملة

اليهود فقال قيصر ومن هم هولا اجاب بيلاطس وقال هم هيرودس

وارشيلاوس وفيلبس وانس وقيافا وكل مجمع اليهود ⁘ فقال قيصر ولما

٢٠ تحققت ارادة مشبه اوليك اجاب بيلاطس وقال انها ايه السيد امة

مشغبة وليس تخضع لقوتك قال قيصر فكان ينبغى لك عند ما اسلموه

Tisch. p. 451 اليك ان تستوثق منه وتبعث به الي ولا تطيعهم وتصلب رجل صديق

الذى مثل هذه الايات الصالحة قد فعل الذى اخبرت انت فى

page 13 قصتك انك عند ما اردت صلبه كتبت فى لوح هذا يسوع ملك اليهود:

¹ Sic in Cod.

الذين قاموا كثيرة كثيرة يمشون ∴ وانه سلب الجحيم وظهر

للنسوة وقال لـهـم ¹قولوا لتلاميذى يقدمونى الى الجليل ∴

page 5 لان هناك يرونى ∴ وكل تلك الليلة لم يزل النور ظاهر ∴

وكثيرين من اليهود ماتوا فى هوتة تلك الارض وابتلعوا حتى ان

5 كثيرين لم يجدوا للغد ممن فعل بيسوع ما فعل : وان كل

Tisch. r. a.<br>p. 442<br>r. b. p. 449 مجامع اليهود فى اورشليم فروا ولم يظهر منهم احدا فلما رايت هذه

الاشيا المفزعة وبـهـتت نفسى رفعت الى قوتك وفسرت لك جميع ما

Paradosis<br>Pilati فعلوا اليهود بيسوع وبعثت الى ملكك ✿ فلما وصلت هذه الرسالة

الى قيصر وقريت بحضرة الكل صاروا مبهوتين عند ما ²سمعوا ان

10 بخطية بلاطس كانت الزلزلة والظلمة على جميع المسكونة ∴

وان قيصر امتلا غيظا ووجه فرسان لياتوه بلاطس فى وثاق فلما

Tisch.<br>p. 450 اتوا به الى مدينة رومية وسمع قيصر ان بلاطس قد قدم: جلس

فى موضع هيكل الالهة مع جميع اشرافه وكل روساه وامر ان يقدم

بلاطس ويوقف قدامه فقال له قيصر لماذا استجريت على مثل هذه

15 الامور الكـافـرة ∴ وانـت قد رايت فى هذا الرجل هذه العلامات

واستجريت على هذا الفعل السو واهـلـكـت كل العالم بخطيتك ∴

اجاب بلاطس قايلا يا لقيصر ضابط الكل انا برى من هذا كله وانما

سبب هـذا: مـلـة اليـهـود فقال قيصر ومن هولا قال بلاطس هم

هرودس. وارشيلاوس. وفلبس. وانس. وقيافا. وكل مجمع اليهود ∴

20 فقال قيصر ولماذا اتبعت ارادة هوليك ∴ قال بلاطس لانها امة شغبة

وما تخضع لقوتك. قال قيصر فكان ينبغى لك عند ما اسلموه

Tisch.<br>p. 451 اليك ان تستوثق منه وتوجه به الي ولا تطيعهم وتصلب رجل صديق

الذى قد فعل مثل هذه الايات الصالحة الذى وصفتهم فى كتابك

وانك عند ما اردت صلبه كتبت فى لوح هذا يسوع ملك اليهود

¹ Sic in Cod.        ² Cod. سمعوان

وعند ما تكلم بهذا القيصر وسمى باسم يسوع كل جميع اصنام الالهة
وقعت وانكسرت وصارت مثل التراب والغبار فى ذلك الموضع الذى كان
فيه القيصر قاعد مع جميع جلساه وانه الجمع الذى كان واقف حول
قيصر فزعوا وارتعدوا ومضى كل واحد منهم الى بيته بفزع شديد
متعجبين مما كان وان قيصر امر ان يستوثق من بيلاطس الى الغد ٥
حتى يتعرف امر ايسوع بفحص. وللغد قعد القيصر مع جميع جلساه

page 14
Tisch. p. 452

واتوا بيلاطس ثم ابتدا يسايله قايلا اخبرنى بالحق يا ¹رشيع انك ¹برشع
فعلك الذى استجريت به على يسوع فقد ظهر شر فعلك لان بسببه
سقطت الالهة فاخبرنى من هو هذا المصلوب الذى اسمه اهلك
الالهة اجاب بيلاطس وقال التذكرة التى رفعت اليك فيه هى حق ١٠
فانا قد قنعت من الفعال الذى فعل انه هو اكبر من كل الالهة
التى نعبد فقال له قيصر فلماذا انت تفعل مثل هذا على يسوع
وانت لم تجهله لو لا انك اردت السو بملكى اجاب بيلاطس وقال

page 15

من اجل خطية اليهود مخالفى الناموس فعلت هذا وان قيصر
غضب وصنع مشورة مع جلساه وامر ان تكتب على اليهود قضية ١٥

Tisch. p. 453

هكذا الى لوقيانوس المتقدم فى بلدة المشرق افزع من اجل الجرة
التى كانت فى هذا الزمان فى اليهود المخالفين الساكنين فى
بيت المقدس وما حولها من المدن ومن اجل افعالهم المخالفة
للناموس انهم دانوا وصلبوا لاله يقال له ايسوع حتى ان من خطيتهم
اظلم العالم كله وكاد ان يصير الى الهلاك فانا اريد ان تجمع ٢٠
عساكر وتصير الى ثم وتضع عليهم الشى وبهذه القضية تبيدهم

page 16

وتستعبدهم فى كل البلاد وتنفيهم من بيت المقدس فلما بلغت هذه
الرسالة القضية الى بلاد المشرق وسمع لوقيانوس واطاع بحرف لامر

¹ These are Syriac words.

فلما تكلم بهذا قيصر وسمى اسم يسوع جميع اصنام الالهة تواقعت

page 6

وتكسرت وصارت مثل التراب والغبار فى ذلك الموضع الذى كان فيه

قيصر جالس مع جميع وزراه وان الجمع الذى كان واقف حول

قيصر فزعوا وارتعدوا وانصرفوا الى منازلهم فزعين متعجبين مما كان

5 وان قيصر امر ان يستوثقوا من بلاطس الى الغد حتى يتعرف امر

يسوع بفحص· وللغد جلس قيصر مع جميع جلساه واحضروا

Tisch.
P. 452

بلاطس فابتدا يسله قايلا اخبرنى بالحق يا ¹رشيع انك ¹برشع فعلت

الذى استجريت تفعله على يسوع والان قد ظهر شر فعلك لان من

اجله تواقعت الالهة فاخبرنى من هو هذا المصلوب الذى اسمه اهلك

10 الالهة قال بلاطس التذكرة التى رفعت اليك من اجله هى حق وانا

فقد قنعت من الفعال الذى فعل انه هو اكبر من كل الالهة

التى نعبد فقال له قيصر فلماذا انت تفعل مثل هذا على يسوع

وانت لم تجهله لو لا انك اردت السو بملكى قال بلاطس من اجل

خطية اليهود وكثرة شغبهم مخالفى الناموس فعلت هذا ÷ وان

15 قيصر غضب وصنع مشورة مع جلساه وامر ان تكتب على اليهود

Tisch.
P. 453

قضية هكذا الى لوقيانوس المتقدم فى بلد المشرق افزع من اجل

الجرة ²الذى كانت فى هذا الزمان من اليهود المخالفين سكان

بيت المقدس وما هو حولها من المدن ومن اجل فعلهم المخالف

للناموس لانهم ³لاله يقال له يسوع دانوا وصلبوا حتى ان من

20 خطيتهم اظلم العالم كله وكاد ان يصير الى الهلاك ÷ فشا ان

تجمع عساكر وصير الى هناك وضع عليهم الشى وبهذه القضية

تبيدهم وتستعبدهم فى كل البلدان وتنفيهم من بيت المقدس ÷ فلما

بلغت هذه القضية الى بلاد المشرق سمع واطاع لوقيانوس بحروف لامر

---

¹ These are Syriac words.      ² Sic in Cod.

³ Cod. لا اله

Tisch.
p. 454 قيصر فتصير وسبى جميع امة اليهود والذين ١تبقوا فيما بين الامم

امر ان يستعبدوا الى هذا اليوم حتى انه بلغ قيصر ما فعل لوقيانوس

باليهود واعجبه جدا وايضا وضع ٢قيـصر يسال بيلاطس عن امر

ايسوع فعند ذلك امر ان يقطع راسه لانه مديده على يسوع الاله

وان بيلاطس وهو جاز الى موضع القتل صلى بسكوت وقال يا رب ٥

لا تهلكنى مع اليهود الخبثا لانى انا لم امد عليك يداى لو لا الامة

page ١٧ الملعونة المخالفة للناموس اقاموا علي شغب وانت تعلم يا رب انى

بجهل فعلت فلا تهلكنى بهذه الخطية. بل ولا تحقد علي ولا على امتك

ابرقلة الواقفة معى فى وقت موتى التى علمتها ان تتنبى عند الوقت

Tisch.
p. 455 التى اردت ان تصلب ولا بخطيتى تدين لى ولها ولكن اغفر لنا يا رب ١٠

وفى نصيب الصديقين احسبنا وعند ما تم صلاته اتاه صوت من السما

قايلا الان يعطوك الطوبى يا بيلاطس كل الاجيال وقبايل والامم لانك

تممت اقاويل الانبيا من اجلى وانت شاهد فى قدومى الثانى وساتظهر

page ١٨ اذا اردت ان ادين اثنا عشر سبط اسرايل والذين لم يقروا ولم يامنوا

باسمى وحينيذ قطع السياف راس بيلاطس وان ملاك الرب قبله ١٥

فلما ابضرت امراته ابرقلة الملاك امتلت فرحا واسلمت روحها ايضا

ودفنت مع زوجها فلربنا ايسوع المسيح التسبحة والعظمة والملك

الان والى دهر الداهرين. امين ::

١ Cod. تبقون.  ٢ Sic in Cod.

Tisch.
P. 454
page 7

قيصر فخرج وسبى جميع امة اليهود والذين تبقوا فيما بين الامم

امر ان يستعبدوا الى يوما هذا حتى انه بلغ قيصر ما فعل لوقيانوس

باليهود فاعجبه ذلك جدا وان قيصر جعل يسل بلاطس عن امر

يسوع وبعد ذلك امر ان يقطع راسه اذ مديده على يسوع الاله :.

5 وان بلاطس وهو ذاهب الى موضع القتل صلى بسكوت وقال يا ربى

لا تهلكنى مع اليهود الخبثا لانى انا لم امد عليك يداى لو لا الامة

المخالفة للناموس اقاموا علي شغب وانت عارف يا رب انى بجهل

فعلت فلا تهلكنى بهذه الخطية ولا تحقد علي ولا على امتك ابرقلة

الواقفة مع فى وقت موتى لانك الهمتها النبوة فى الوقت الذى

Tisch.
P. 455

10 هويت ان تصلب ولا بخطيتى تدين لجميعا: ولكن اغفر لنا يا رب

ومع احباك صيرنا فلما تم صلاته اذا صوت من السما قايلا الان

يا بلاطس يعطوك الطوبى كل الاجيال وقبايل الامم لانك تممت

اقاويل الانبيا من اجلى :. وانت شاهد فى قدومى الثانى وساتظهر

اذا اردت ادين اثنا عشر سبط اسرايل والذين لم يقرون ويومنون

15 باسمى :. وحينيذ قطع السياف راس بلاطس وان ملاك الرب قبله

فلما ابصرت امراته ابرقلة الملاك امتلت فرحا واسلمت روحها ايضا

ودفنت مع زوجها فلربنا يسوع المسيح التسبحة والعظمة والملك من

الان والى دهر الداهرين. امين :.

قصة تعرف اقليمس

بوالديه واخوته من قبل

بطرس الرسول

من النسخة القديمة الموجودة

فى دير طور سينا

# RECOGNITIONES
# S. CLEMENTIS ROMANI.

بسم الاب والابن وروح القدس الاه واحد ٠:٠ المسيح الاه قوتى
وعونى ورجاى هذه قصة تعرف اقليمس بوالديه واخوته من قبل
بطرس الرسول راس السليحين المغبوط بالامانة وهذا تعليم بطرس
السالف المقدس ٠:٠

Recog. Book VI. c. 6
5 عند ما كان فى اطرابلس ٠:٠ ٠:٠ ينبغى ان يوثن الحب فى
الله وعلى الوالدين والبنون لانه سبب كل شى وانه يعسر علينا
ان نعلم ما الله ولاكنا نتيقن بانه الله فلا تظنوا بانكم مومنين

VI. 8
اذا انتم كنتم بلا معمودية لانه منها شخص من الرحمة موجود فى

Homiliae XI. c. 26
الما عارف بالمعمدين فى اسر ¹الثالوث المقدس المنجى من العذاب
10 المستانف فلذلك اسرعوا الى الما فانه هو وحده القادر ان يطفى
ذلك النار فلما ان قال هذا انطلق الجماعة فكان عند ما تمت
لى ثلثة اشهر معه انا اقليمس امرنى ان اصوم ثلثة ايام فعند ذلك

VI. 15
صرنا عند منابع ²امياه على ساحل البحر فعمدنى هنالك و لمرابلس

page 2
معى الرجل الذى اضافنا ٠:٠ ثم انه سواه اسقف على اطرابلس واثنا
15 عشر قسيس مع شماسة ثم انه ودع ²ودع اهل اطرابلس وخرج الى

¹ Cod. الثالثوث      ² Sic in Cod.

انطاكية ¹الشام ۞ وكان سبب لقاى اياه هاكذا عند ما كنت فى

مدينة رومية فى ²حداثة سنى كنت كثير معنت بالعفة والصلاح

وذكر الموت والفكر فى النفس هل هى ام ميتة وهل هذا العالم

كان له مبتدا ام لا وهل يعطل ام لا ۞ فعند ما كنت مفكر فى

5 هولاى لم ازل ³اراتب موضع الفلاسفة والحكما فلم ³اكون اجد شيا

من الباب اكثر من امر محتال معطل فرايت ان اصير الى مصر عند

العرافين بالاموات فلما ان فكرت بهذا اذا بخبر قد اشيع فى ملك

طباريوس عن رجل فى ارض يهودا مبشر بملك الله الازلى ويثبت

ذلك بجرايح كثيرة فلما كان هذا هاكذا اذا برنابا قد قدم

10 الى رومية يكرز المسيح فكانت الحكما تستهزى به ۞ فعند ذلك

انا عرفت له بمعنى البر وتقلدت حجته فرفضت بهولايك مثل

الكلاب الذى لم يقبلوا كلام الخلاص فاخذت برنابا واضفته عندى

وكنت اسمع منه القول فلما ان هم بالخروج الى ارض يهودا

خرجت معه وفى خمسة عشر يوما صرت الى قيسارية فاخبرت

15 بان بطرس فيها وهو يريد مجادلة سمعان فى الغد فعند ما صرت

الى منزله ادخلنى برنابا اليه فقبلنى بطرس بمودة كثيرة وفرح كثير

عن ما اوليت برنابا فى رومية فاكثر لى الدعا وامرنى ان اصير

اليه وهو يريد المسير الى رومية فلما اوعدته بذلك سالته عن النفس

وعن العالم فاوضح لى بالاستقصا باقتصاد الجهل الدخيل على الناس

20 من قبل الخطيه وهو الذى غشى عقول الناس مثل الدخان وشرح

لى قدوم المسيح والنهضة الى الحياة ۞ وفى الغد اذا بزكا قد قدم

وهو قايل بان سمعان قد ³وخر المجادلة الى سبع ايام يستكمل

بطرس تعليمه لنا عن معرفة العالم كمثل ما اعطته روح القدس ۞

فبعد هذا صرنا الى اطرابلس فى الموضع الذى فيه اعتمدت ومن

Left margin references:
- I. 1
- Hom. I. 1
- Hom. I. 3
- I. 5. Hom. I. 5
- I. 6. Hom. I. 6
- I. 7. Hom. I. 9
- page 3
- I. 10. Hom. I. 13
- I. 12
- I. 13. Hom. I. 16
- I. 14. Hom. I. 17
- page 4. I. 20

---

¹ Cod. السام     ² Cod. حداث     ³ Sic in Cod.

هناك ارسل بطرس نقيطا والقيلاس مع اخرين الى الادقية وامرهم

ان ينتظروه عند باب المدينة ∵ فاما انا وهو فصرنا الى انطرطوس

فشكرته لانه خلفنى معه فقال لى ان انا جلبتك الى موضع تبتاع   Hom. XII. 4

لنا فيه حوايج هل تموت فاستجبت انا وقلت له انت لى بدل   VII. 4

ابى وامى واخوتى قد صرت لى سبب لمعرفة الحق ∵ فانت ساويتنى ٥

باهل الكبار فكيف تجعلنى فى موضع الخدم ∵ فاستجاب بطرس وهو   VII. 5. Hom. XII. 5-6.

مازح وقال لى هل تظن انك قد صرت عبدا ∵ فمن يحفظ   page 5

على خلعى وشوارى ومن يعد لى الاطبخة الكثيرة المحتاجين   VII. 6

الى الطباخين وذلك بكثرة الحيل التى احتيلت للناس المونثين

فى رضا الشهوة التى هى الشبع الكثير واكتسى به من الاستكثار ١٠

فلا تظن انك تتعرف بشى من هذا اذ انت معى ∵ لانى ما

اصيب الا اقصد ما يكون من الخبز وشى من زيتون مع بقل

قليل واما كسوتى كلها فهو هذا الخلق الذى ترى عليه والى

غيره لا احتاج لان عقلى يرى الخيرات الدهرية ولا يلتفت الى

شى مما هونا ∵ وانا منك متعجبا لانك رجل مربى فى نعيم ١٥

العالم فزهدت بذلك كله وقنعت باليسير من الامور ∵ واما انا   page 6

واخى اندراوس تربينا باليتم والفقر والشقا واعتدنا التعب ونحتمل

النصب من اجل ذلك فانا اصبر منك على التعب وعلى خدمتك

انت لنفسك ∵ فعند ما سمعت هذا منه اقشعرت من ذلك واعتبرت   VII. 7. Hom. XII. 7

عند ما سمعت هذا من رجل لا تسواه الدنيا فدمعت عينى فعند ٢٠

ما رانى باكى قال لى لماذا دمعت عينيك فاستجبت انا قايل ما

اجرمت اليك لتسمعنى هذا الكلام فقال بطرس ∵ ان كنت قد

اسيت بانى قلت ان اخدمك فانت اجدر ان تكون قد اسات بديا

لما لم ترى ذلك ولا سوى فى هذا اما انا فيشبه ذلك ان افعله

بك ∵ فاما انت ايه الرسول من الله مخلصا لانفسنا لا يشبه ذلك ٢٥   page 7

ان تفعله انت فاستجاب بطرس اذن قبلت منك القول لولا

ان ربنا القادم لخلاص العالم الذى هو وحده الذى له الحسب

احتمل الخدمة كيما يقنعنا ان لا نستحى بخدمتنا لاخوتنا ∴ وهو

وضا ¹ارجلى وايدى قايل هاكذا افعلوا باخوتكم فقلت له انا اقليمس

5 ان انا ظننت انى اقهرك بالكلام فقد سفهت ولاكنى اشكر الله

page 8
Hom. XII. 8

الذى جعلك فى موضع والدين فقال لى بطرس هل يكون لك

VII. 8

احد من قرابة فقلت له فى جنسى رجال هم اشراف يقاربون لقيصر

الملك ∴ وهو زوج والدتى ذو حسب ومنها صرنا ثلثة اولاد ∴ توم

قبلى كما اخبرنى والذى انى لا اعرفهم ولا لوالدتى الا ذكر

10 ضعيف وبعدهما ولدتنى امى وكان اسمها مثاذية ووالدى كان اسمه

فسطنيان واخوتى فسطس وفسطنيانوس فلما صرت فى خمسة سنين

رات والدتى فى احلامها رويا كما حدثنى ابى من بعد ذلك ان

لم تاخذ المرة ولديها من ساعتها وتخرج من رومية وتسافر عشر

page 9

سنين والا فسوف تعطب هى وهما فاما ابى عندما سمع هذا

VII. 9
Hom. XII. 9

15 حملهم فى سفينة بزاد سرى مع خدم كثير وارسلهم لينقبوا فى

اثيناس وامسكنى انا وحدى قبله ليتعزانى مغنظا بذلك ∴ فلما ان

مضى سنة بعد ذلك ارسل ابى الى اثيناس مال ونفقات ولكيما يعرف

حالهم فمضوا الرسل ولم يرجعوا ∴ وفى السنة الثالثة ارسل اخرين

فى ذلك فانطلقوا وقدموا فى السنة الرابعة يخبروا انهم لم يصيبوا

20 الغلامين ولا والدتهم فانهم لم يصلوا الى ²اثيناس البتة ∴ ولم

VII. 10
Hom. XII. 10

يجدوا لهم اثر فلما ان سمع والدى هذا حزن حزن شديد وتحير

page 10

جدا الا يدرى كيف ياجد ولا اين [يب]لكيهم ∴ فنزل الى ساحل

البحر وانا معه فجعل يسل النواتية عن كل موضع غرقت فيه

السفن من اربع سنين هل يكون احدهم راى مرة غريقة مع

¹ Cod. رجلى     ² Cod. الى ثيناس

A. P.

صبيانها ولم يقع على يقين الامر لانه ليس احد يستقصى سعة
البحر ٠٠ عند ذلك خلفنى فى رومية ووكل بى وكلا وانا يوميذ
ابن اثنا عشر سنة وركب من رومية فى سفينة وانطلق الى
المواضع يطلبهم فحينذ لم اسمع له خبر ولا كتاب ولا ادرى حى
هو ام ميت مع انى اظن انه قد توفى فقد مضت له اليوم ٥

page ١١
VII. ١١
Hom. XII. ١١

عشرين سنة منذ فارقنى : فلما ان سمع هذا بطرس دمعت عينيه
من الشفقة وقال للذين كانوا معه من المومنين ابتلى بما اصيب
ابو هذا ٠٠ يعنى بالمومنين الذين هم غير الامم البطالة الذين
يتبلون هاهنا بلا ثواب فى الاخرة ٠٠ لان الذين يجربون هاهنا
من المومنين فلتركان ذنوبهم يبتلون به ٠٠ فلما قال هذا بطرس ١٠

VII. ١٢
Hom. XII. ١٢

استجاب واحد ممن كان حاضر قدام كل وطلب الى بطرس
قايل اذا كان بالغداة سيرتنا الى جزيرة ارواذ فى البحر حتى
تنظر اليها ٠٠ فان هنالك عمودين عظيمين من اعواد الكرم والنظر

page ١٢

اليها عجيب فاذن لنا بطرس ان نذهب وقال لنا اذا انتم بلغتم فلا
تنطلقوا كلكم الى الموضع العجيب جميعا لكيما لا تصيبكم افة ٠٠ ١٥
فسرنا واتينا الى الجزيرة فانحدرنا من السفينة حيث كانا العمودين
فجعل كل واحد منا يتلفت الى بعض الاعاجيب التى كانت

VII. ١٣
Hom. XII. ١٣

هنالك ٠٠ فاما بطرس عند ما صار الى العمد اذا بامراة قاعدة خارج
الابواب تسل صدقة ٠٠ فلما ان ابصرها بطرس قال لها ايه المرة ماذا
ينقصيك من اعضاك حتى اذا ¹صرت الى هذه القماة لتستعطى ولا ٢٠
[تستكثر] بما وهبه الله لك من عمل يديك كثنى ولى به الخبز
يوم ببوم ²فتنهدت المرة وقالت يا ليت كانت لى يدين يقدران

page ١٣

على الخدمة والعمل ولاكنهما فى شبه يدين وهن ميتات وذلك
لما نهشتهما باسنانى فاستجاب بطرس وقال وما هو السبب الذى

² Cod. فاتناهدت ¹ Cod. صرتى

الجاك ان تفعلين هذا فقالت المرة سببه هو العجز فقط لو كانت

لى جراة او قوة كنت قد طرحت نفسى من جبل او فى عمق

VII. 14
Hom. XII. 14
واسترحت من الاحزان والغموم التى آلي جدفت بى قال بطرس

فالذين يقتلون انفسهم هل يخلصون من العذاب ام يصبرون الى

5 اكثر منه فى الجحيم مع الانفس الذى فعلت هاكذا لقتلها اياها

فقالت المرة يا ليت انى ايقنت بان فى الجحيم انفس حية لكيما

page 14
اصير هنالك وابصر احباى ولو كنت بالعذاب ∴ فقال بطرس وما هو

هذا الذى يحزنك يا مرة اخبرينى فان انا علمت سوف اشفيك

واقنعك بان فى الجحيم انفس حية واعطيك حيلة لا تحتاجى

VII. 15
Hom. XII. 15
10 معها الى غرق ولا الى غيره فتخرجى من الجسد بلا عذاب ففرحت

بالميعاد وجعلت تحدثه قايلة انى امراة كنت ¹ذو حسب فابتنى بى

رجل شريف ذو خطر قريب لقيصر الملك وصار لى منه ولدين تومان

وكان لى ولد اخر غيرهما فبعد ذلك عشقنى اخو زوجى فكنت

اصرفه يحى للعفة ولم اكن انهى الى زوجى حركته ¹السوا لى

15 فرايت ان لا اطبعه وادنس فراش زوجى معما اتشب العداوة بينهما

page 15
فيصير ذلك لى عار الى جميع جنسى فاجمعت على الخروج من

المدينة بابنى الى زمان قليل حتى يهدا ذلك الهوا الردى ويتقصى

VII. 16
Hom. XII. 16
عنى الادا فخلفت ابنى الاخر قبل ابيه ليتعذى به واحلمت بحلم

كانى رايت منام ليلا قايلا لى ايه المرة اخرجى مع ولديك من

20 هاهنا الى زمان اعلمك فيه ²رجوعك والا فسوف تهلكين مع زوجك

واولادك ∴ ولذلك فعلت فلما حدثت زوجى بهذا قشعر من ذلك

ثم قام وحملنى فى سفينة مع اولادى وخدم كثيرين فاموال

كثيرة فارسلنا الى اثيناس فلما ان سرنا فى البحر قامت علينا

الروامس وانتشبت الامواج وغرقنا ليلا فغرق كل من كان معنا

¹ Sic in Cod.      ² Cod. رجعوك

page 16 وطرحت انا الشقية مع الموج الى جانب صحرة واشتبكت بها رجا

ان اجد اولادى احيا لذلك لم ¹اكون اقذف بنفسى الى العمق

واستريح فقد كان هذا لعمرى حينيذ خفيف لما احدق بى من

VII. 17
Hom. XII. 17
الحزن ∴ فلما ان غشانى الصبح جعلت التفت والتمس اولادى

الغرقى واندبهم وانوح مع بكا من عند ما لم ارى منهم احد ولا 5

اجسادهم الغريقة فلما راونى اهل الموضع رحمونى وسترونى ثم

انهم التمسوا اولادى فى العمق فلم يصيبوهم فاتين البي نسوة

معزيات لى وكانوا يذكروا من المصايب ومن الاحزان ما ابتلين

به كمثل ما اصابنى وكان ذلك مما يزيدنى الحزن بانه لم تكون

10 مصايب غيرى مما تعزينى ∴ فعزمن علي ان اصير اليهما فصرت

page 17 الى مرة فقيرة لما عزمت علي ان اصير اليها وقالت لى كان لى

زوج توفى ومات غريق فى البحر وخلفنى يوميذ شابه فى سنى

ومن حينيذ لم اعرف رجل وان كثيرين دعونى الى التزويج فاثرت

العفة والتقيا على زوجى فهلمى ونصير فى حياة واحدة ومعاش واحد

15 فساكنتها لحفظها مودة زوجها ∴ فبعد ذلك اشتكيت يدى فيبست

VII. 18
Hom. XII. 18
والمرة مساكنتى تجعلت ملقاة هنالك فى البيت فانا حينيذ من

زمان قاعدة هاهنا سايلة الصدقة لى ولصاحبتى فقد اشرحت لك

امرى وقصتى فتم لى الان موعودك لكيما تعطينى العلاج الذى

به يمكنى الوحا من هذه الدنيا مع صاحبتى ∴ فلما قالت المرة هذا

VII. 19
Hom. XII. 19
20 اكثر بطرس بالفكر وهو حينيذ قايم فقدمت انا اقليمس الى بطرس

page 18 وقلت له ايه المعلم الصالح اين كنت وانا منذ حين التمسك اى

شى تامرنا ان نفعل فقال اسبق وانتظرنى فى السفينة ففعلت كما

امرنى فاعاد المسلة على المرة وقال لها اخبرنى بجنسك ومدينتك

واولادك واسماهم وانا اعطيك الدوا فلم تكون المرة تريد ان تخبره

¹ Sic in Cod. *passim.*

بذلك فجعلت تخبره بغير الحق لتاخذ الدوا وقالت له انى مرة
مـن افسس وزوجى مـن سقلية وابدلت اسما اولادها فنظر بطرس
انها صادقة فقال لها انى لقد ظننت بانه سوف يصير اليك اليوم
حظ مـن السرور لانى حسبتك مرة انا عارف بامورها فاقسمت عليه

5 المرة قايلة انا اسلك لما اخبرتنى بالذى عندك فانه لا اظن ان

VII. 20
Hom. XII. 20

page 19

فى النسا واحدة اشقى منى فجعل بطرس يحدثها بالحق ويقول ان
معى [1]شاب لحقى فى طلبة المعرفة باليقين بالله وهو من رومية
مع واخبرنى عن اب كان له واخوين تومين وزعم ان امه كما
اخبره ابوه انها ارت بالمنام ان تخرج من رومية مع ولديها لكيما

10 لا تهلك مع زوجها فخرجت ولا يدرى الى ماذا صار امرها وان ابوه

VII. 21
Hom. XII. 21

خرج فى طلبها فغاب خبره ايضا ولا يدرى ما كان منه فلما قال
هذا بطـرس وقعت المرة مغشى عليها فتقدم بطرس فامسك بيدها
وقال لها ثقى واطمانى واصدقينى ما بك عند ذلك كانها استفاقت
من الغشوة ومسحت على [2]وجهها وقالت اين هذا الشاب الذى قلت

15 لى فقال بطرس اخبرينى انتى بديا بامرك وانا اريك اياه فقالت
انا ام هذا الغلام قال بطرس هل اسمه قالت اقليمس اسمه فقال

page 20

بطرس هو الفتى الذى قبيل وامرته ان ينتظرنى فى السفينة فخرت
ساجدة وقالت اسرع بدا الى السفينه لترينى ابنى الوحيد بانى ان
انا رايته فقد رايت اولادى الغرقى هاهنا فقال لها بطرس انى فاعل

20 بك هذا ولاكن اذا انتى رايته فاسكتى حتى تنزل من الجزيرة

VII. 22
Hom. XII. 22

فقالت المـرة كذلك انا فاعلة فامسك بيدها بطرس وادناها الى
السفينة فلما رايته انا ماسك بيد مرة ابتسمت ثم انى وقرته عن
ذلك وجعلت ان اهدى المرة فلما ان امسكت بيدها صاحت صوت
كبير باكية وعانقتنى فجعلت تقبلنى فانا لم اكون اعرف

VII. 23
Hom. XII. 23

page 21

الامر ظننت بانها مصابة او موسوسة فدفعتها عني فقال بطرس لما

يا بنى دفعت عنك والدتك فلما ان سمعت هذا منه بانها والدتى

اضطرب قلبى ودمعتا ¹اعينى وطرحت نفسى عليها وحر قلبى اليها

واخذنى البكا من الفرح والشفقة وقبلتها واقبلوا الينا جميع الناس

الذين كانوا هنالك مسرعين ينظرون الى المرة السايلة كيف عرفت 5

ابنها فلما ان اردنا الخروج من الجزيرة قالت لى امى يا بنى

الحبيب الواجب علي ان اودع المرة ²التى قبلتنى وهى ايضا مرة

مخلعة مطروحة فى المنزل فلما ان سمع بطرس عجب من عقل

المرة وامر ان تحمل المرة المخلعة بالسرير وياتوا بها اليه فلما

قربوها قال بطرس والناس سامعين ان كنت انا رسول المسيح 10

الان يامنون هولاى ان الله هو الوحيد خالق كل شى ³فالتقوم

هذه المرة صحيحة فلما ان قال هذا بطرس قامت المرة صحيحة

page 22

وسجدت لبطرس وسالته عن هذه الامور فاقنعها وعلمت يقين الامر

VII. 24
Hom. XII. 24

فلما سمعوا جماعة الناس عجبوا عجب كثير وكلمهم بطرس كلام

فى الدين وفى اخرة قال من اراد ان يستمع اليقين بالله عن 15

خلاص نفسه فليصير الى انطاكية فانى قد وهلت الاقامة بها ثلثة

اشهر فانه اوجب من الغربة فى تجارة ارباح الدنيا طلب خلاص

الانفس وربح الاخرة فبعد كلام بطرس للناس ناولت المرة التى

ابراها بطرس الف درهم ووكلت بها رجل صالح وكافيت النسوة

³الذين كلة يعرفن امى وانا سرنا الى انطرطوس مع بطرس وامى 20

VII. 25
Hom. XIII. 1

والباقيين فلما انتهينا الى المنزل سالتنى امى قايلة كيف حال

page 23

ابوك يا بنى فقلت لها من حين خرج فى طلبك لم يعرف له اثرا

فعند ما سمعت هذا تنهدت وحزنت فمن بعد يوم خرجنا الى

الادقية فلما ان قدمنا اليها فاذا قدام الابواب تلميذين لبطرس نقيطا

---

¹ Cod. عينى    ² Cod. الذى    ³ Sic in Cod.

<sup></sup>وجولاس <sup>ا</sup>ولقيونا وصيرونا الى المنزل فعند ما ارى بطرس الموضع

موافق احب ان يقم هنالك عشرة ايام فسالنى نقيطا واجولاس قايلين

من هذه المرة فقلت لهم هذه هى والدتى <sup>ا</sup>الذى اذن الله لى

VII. 26
Hom. XIII. 2

بمعرفتها <sup>٢</sup>بعناية سيدى بطرس فعند ما قلت هذا اوضح لهما بطرس

5   يقين الامر كيف كان كمثل ما اخبرته انا عن امى كمثل ما

VII. 28

سمع هو منها وهو الذى اهدانا الى معرفة بعضنا بعض فلما قال

page 24

هذا بطرس عجبوا جدا عند ما سمعوا بطرس عن المرة وذكرها

Hom. XIII. 3

ابنيها فسطس وفسطنيانوس وبهتوا من الحديث ∴ فقالوا هل نرى هذا

منام هو او حقا ان لم <sup>ا</sup>نكون موسوسين فهو حقا ∴ فضربوا على

10   وجوههم وقالوا نحن هم فسطس وفسطنيانوس فاوجزت قلوبنا عند

ما ابتدات بالحديث وامسكنا حتى نسمع انتها الحديث لانه كثير

ما يكون من الامور مشابهة بعضها لبعض ∴ فهذه لعمرى امنا وهذا

هو اخونا ∴ فلما ان قالوا هذا اعتنقونى ببكا كثير وقبلونى فدخلوا

الى امنا فاصابوها نايمة ∴ فقال لهم بطرس لا تيقظوها لكيلا ينقلب

VII. 29
Hom. XIII. 4

15   عليها بغتة حراك السرور فتصغر اليها نفسها فلما ان استيقظت امنا

اخذ بطرس يقول لها اعلمك ايها المرة بديننا وايماننا بالله نحن

page 25

نومن باله واحد خالق كل هذا العالم الذى يرى ونحن نحفظ

وصاياه ونقدس ونبر الوالدين ∴ ونحيا حياة زكية ولا نباشر الامم

فى طعام ولا فى شراب الا ان يعتمدون بسم الاب والابن وروح

20   القدس ∴ فان كان اب او ام او مرة او ابن او اخ غير معتمد

لا نواكله فلا تغتمى لان ابنك على هذا الا ان تصيرى مثله ∴

VII. 30
Hom. XIII. 5

فلما ان سمعت هذا قالت وما الذى ينبغى من ان اعتمد اليوم

وان اصير الى ذلك لان نفسى قد بغضت الهة الزور لانهم يلهموا

غير العفة التى من اجلها هربت من رومية مع اولادى فسطس

لعناية      <sup>٢</sup> Cod.          <sup>١</sup> Sic in Cod.

وفسطنيان فلما ان قالت هذا امنا لم يصبروا اخوتى نقيطا واجولس

ولاكنهم اسر وعانقوها فقبلوها ٠٠ فقالت المرة ما هذا الامر قال

بطرس ايها المرة احضرى عقلك هولا هم اولادك فسطس وفسطنيانوس

الذين كنت تظنين انهما قد غرقان فى البحر كيف هوذا هما

احيا وقدامك ابتلعهم البحر فى جوف من الليل وكيف يقال ٥

للواحد نقيطا والاخر اجولس ٠٠ يخبرونا هم الان حتى نعلم نحن

وانتى فلما قال هذا بطرس وقعت المرة مغشى عليها من الفرح

فاقمناها بتعب شديد فعند ما قعدت قالت لنا اطلب اليكم ¹يا

اولادى الاحبا اخبرونى ما الذى حدث بكم فى تلك الليلة ٠٠

فقال اخى نقيطا اخبرك يا امتاه انه فى تلك الليلة ١٠

عند ما انكسرت بنا السفينة حملونا فى القارب يردون بنا

البيع فقدفوا بنا الى الارض ²واتوا بنا الى قيسارية فعذبونا

هنالك بالجوع والضرب لكيما لا نتكلم شى لا يوافقهم ٠٠ فابدلوا اسمانا

وباعونا لمرة يهودية اسمها يسطة فاشترتنا وادبتنا فعند ما عقلنا صرنا

الى يقين الامانة بالله فابتدانا بالمجادلة والمحاورة لتبكت طغيان ١٥

جميع الامم وتعلمنا اقوال الحكم لننفض به الحكم والحجج البطالة

فصاحبنا رجل ساحر يقال له سمعان فصرنا معه بجدا المودة فكاد

ان يطغينا فبلغينا ان فى ارض يهودا نبيا وكل من يومن به يحيا

بلا حزن ولا موت فظنناه انه سمعان فبعد ذلك لقينا تلميذ لمولانا

بطرس يقال له زكى فوعظنا جدا وحدرنا من الساحر وقربنا الى ٢٠

بطرس فهدانا الى معرفة الحق ٠٠ ونحن نطلب الى الله ان يساويك

ياهل للنعمة ³الذى صرنا اليها لكيما نمتلى من النعمة فى بعضنا

بعض ٠٠ هذا هو السبب الذى ³ظننتى بانا قد غرقنا فى تلك

الليلة وظنننا نحن ايضا بانك قد ³هلكتى فى البحر ٠٠ فلما قال

¹ Cod. ياولادى.          ² Cod. واتو.          ³ Sic in Cod.

هذا نقيطا جرت امنا لبطرس وقالت اسلك واطلب اليك ان تعمدنى

لان لا اعدم يوم واحد من مخالطة اولادى فطلبنا اليه بذلك

VII. 38<br>Hom. XIV. 1 فامرها ان تصوم ثلثة ايام ثم انه من بعد ذلك اعمدها فى البحر

بمحضر اولادها فاصبنا معها الطعام: وسررنا بذلك نسبح الله وتعليم

5 بطرس وللذى صرنا اليه من معرفة امنا وعلمنا بان العفة ¹للامر

VIII. 1 page 29 سبب خلاص فبعد ذلك اليوم اخذنا بطرس الى المينا واستحمنا

Hom. XIV. 2 هنالك وصلينا ❖ فاذا بشيخ ثمة قاعد يبصر الينا ويتفرس منا

VIII. 2 الصلاة فبعد ما صلينا اقبل الينا يلومنا ويقول انه كل شى

Hom. XIV. 3 بالبخت يكون وان الدعا والصلاة باطل ❖ فثوينا ثلثة ايام نقنعه

VIII. 8 10 على ان يصرف رايه من هذا الامر وفى ذلك عند كلامنا اياه

كنا ندعيه يا ابتاه وهو كان يدعينا يا اولادى ❖ وذلك كان

تدبير من الله لانه كان ابتدا تعرفنا به هذه الكلمة فقال ²جولس

لى ولنقيطا لما تدعوا هذا الغريب اب فقال لى اخى لا تانف من

ذلك فاكثرنا له فى القول وهو فى رايه ذلك وقال اما الكلام

IX. 32<br>Hom. XIV. 6<br>page 30 15 فقد اقنعنى ولاكنى انا مفكر فى مرتى الذى كان نجمها

وبختها فى الفسق فهربت العشق من اجل العار فغرقت فى البحر

IX. 33<br>Hom. XIV. 7 فقلت له انا اقليمس وكيف تعلم ان المرة لما هربت لم تتزوج

بعض العبيد وانها ماتت انا باليقين اعرف انها لم تتزوج لانها

كانت عفيفة وبعد موتها اخبرنى اخى عنها كيف عشقته بديا

20 وهو بحفاظة اياى واستمساكه بعفته لم يكون يريد يدنس فراشى ❖

فهى الشقية من فزعها منى ومن العار احنالت وليست بملامة لان

هذا قضى عليها اعتلت بمنام راته وقالت لى بانى ان انا

اقمت هاهنا هلكت وولديه ❖ فلما ان سمعت ذلك منها لحرصى

على خلاصها واولادها ارسلتها وامسكت قبلى ابن كان لى ثالث

¹ Cod. للامر.          ² Sic in Cod.

كما انها زعمت انها رات فى احلامها فلما ان سمعت هذا

IX. 34
Hom. XIV. 8

منه قلت لعله هذا هو والدى فدمعت عينى فلما ان وثبوا

page 31

اخوتى يردوا يعانقوه منعهم بطرس وقال لهم اسكتوا حتى يبدو

لى فاستجاب بطرس وقال للشيخ ما اسم ابنك الشاب الاصغر فقال

الشيخ اقليمس اسمه فاجابه بطرس وقال ان انا اوريتك اليوم ٥

مرتك العفيفة مع تلثة اولادها تومن بان العقل العفيف قادر ان

يقهر الحركات البهيمية ∴ وان كلامى الذى كلمتك به فى الله

بانه حق وقال الشيخ كما لا يمكن ان يكون ما اوعدتنى ∴

كذلك ان لا يمكن بلا قضا · قال بطرس انا استشهد هولاى

الحضر بانى اليوم احضر لك مرتك مع ثلثة اولادها حية بعفتها ∴

١٠

والدليل على هذا معرفتى اليقين بالامر اكثر منك وانا اخبرك بكلما

page 32

حدثت لكيما ان تعرف انت ويعلموا هولاى الجماعة كل هذا

فعند ما قال هذا بطرس جعل يقص قايل ان هذا الرجل الذى

IX. 35

تروا ايه الاخوة بكسوته الخلقة هو من اهل رومية من نسب

كبير وحسب شريف قريب لقيصر واسمه فسطنيانوس وتزوج امراة

١٥

شريفة واسمها مشادية ومنها صار له ثلثة اولاد اثنين ¹منهما توم

والاخر اصغرهم اسمه اقليمس وهو هذا وهاذين الاخرين الواحد

اجولاس والاخر نقيطا وقد كان اسماهما بديا واحد فستاس والاخر

فسطنيانوس فلما قال بطرس هذا وسماهم باسماهم تحير الشيخ

وغشى عليه ووقع اولاده عليه يقبلونه ويبكوا يظنوا انه قد مات

٢٠

فبهت الناس من هذا العجب فامرنا بطرس نتحنى عن الشيخ فامسك

page 33 IX. 36

هو بيده واقامه فحدث الناس كل ما دخل عليه من المصايب

وسبب اتفاقهم ∴ فلما علمت بهذا والدتنا اتت مسرعة تصيح وتقول

IX. 37
Hom. VIII. 9

اين زوجى وسيدى فسطنيانوس الذى شقى من اجلى زمان طويل

¹ Sic in Cod.

فى كل مدينة طالبنى وعند ما كانت تصيح هاكذا وثب
الشيخ مسرع اليها بالدموع وعانقوا بعضهم بعض فبعد هذا كله
اطلق بطرس جماعة الناس وامرهم ان ياتوه بالغداة ويسمعوا

IX. 38

الحديث ۞ فاذا برجل من اشراف قدم بامراته واولاده يسلنا ان

page 34

5 نصير الى منزله ولم يقبل بطرس ذلك منه ففى ذلك اذا ¹بابنة
الرجل معتراة بشيطان كان بها منذ عشرين سنه فمن ذلك كانت
مربوطة بالسلاسل محبوسة فى بيت وانفتح البيت بغتة وتهتكت
السلاسل وخرج الشيطان عنها فقدمت الجارية وسجدت لبطرس
وقالت ايه السيد انما جيتك اليوم لحال خلاصى فلا تحزنى ولا
10 لوالدى ۞ فسالهم بطرس عن الجارية فبهتوا والديها عندما ³راوا
السلاسل قد سقطت عنها وطلبتها الى بطرس واشفق عليها بطرس
وامرنا ان نصير الى منزله وفى الغد قدم الينا ابونا وفعل كل
ما امره به بطرس واجرينا الكلام على ان يكون اليقين بالمناظرة
فبعد كلام كثير جدا فى تبكيت الجهالة فامر بطرس لابونا ان لا

X. 1

page 35

15 يمكث على غير الواجب لله فى الدين زمانا بل يتوب لان اجل
الحياة قريب ليس للمشايخ فقط الا وللشباب فانذر الشيخ مع

X. 72

جميع الناس ايام ثم انه اعمد الشيخ بسم الاب والابن وروح
القدس الذى له السبح والمجد الى دهر الداهرين الداهرين امين
يا من يقرا صلى على من كتبه يذكرك الرب بالرحمة امين
20 وجميع المومنين ۞

¹ Cod. بابنت.    ² Cod. لولدى    ³ Cod. روا.

لـ المـنـا و اسمعـنا صاك وصلينا فاداسيع نمه
قاعد بصـر الـنا و بنفرس من الصـلاه فعـد ما
صلينا اقد الـنا ملوصنا و بقو لـ اله كـل شـ بالـهـ
يكون و ارا الـدعا و الصـلاه باكـره فوبا
لله ادام نفعـه عـلى ان يصـرف رابه من صد الامر
و بع داك عند كلامـا اباه كـا ندعـه
با اسناه و صو كاريد عما با اولا د ٥٨ و داك
كارد بر من اله لا نه كان ابدا بعرفـا به صده
الكلمه و عال حولس لـ و لنفـكا لها اند عواهد
العرب ابـ نقال لـ احمـلا انـف من داك
فاكبر باله نى العول و صوبد رابه داك و ذال
اما الكلام فعد انعى و لا كـ ابا معـكر نى مذ
الدبـد كار خبط و خنطـ و العس و صبـ

خبر اكليمنطس بابا رومية

من النسخة الموجودة فى لندن

المكتوبه فى سنة ١٦٠٩

لتجسد المسيح

كتبه ماكاريوس الانطاكي

واخرجه من اللغة الرومية الى اللغة العربية

# RECOGNITIONES CLEMENTIS.

f. 188 a خبر ابينا الجليل فى القديسين اكليمنظس بابا رومية الشهيد

فى الكهنة فهذا المغبوط اكليمنظس كان من مدينة رومية العظمى

نسبه من جنس الملوك عالما جدا وحكيما كما توضح ذلك اقواله

وكتبه لانه تادب بكل حكمة اليونانيين وصار فيلسوفا عجيبا وكان

5 اسم والده فافسطس واسم والدته ماطتيديان وكتب ¹امور الرسل

وغير ذلك وصار اسقفا لرومية وأُنفى من دوماتيانوس الملك فلكن

هلم لنورد يسيرا من الكثير الذى شرحه هذا المغبوط اكليمنظس من

ذلك الذى كتبه الى يعقوب اخا الرب فى الرسالة التى اخبره

فيها عن ساير اموره باستقصا وكيف رجع من ²ضلالته الاولة الى

10 معرفة الله ونكتب ذلك باختصار مع شهادته لانه هكذا كتب فى

مُبتدا رسالته تكون تعرف يا سيدى يعقوب بانى انا ولدت وتربيت

فى رومية وحفظت البثولية من صغر سنى متذكرا دايما للموت   Recogni-<br>tiones, Book I.<br>c. I<br>Homiliæ,<br>Book I. c. I.

وكنت لاجل ذلك فى حزن كثير مفتكرا هكذا فى ذاتى وقايلا

اترى ان نفس الانسان غير مايتة وهل يُوجد عالما غير هذا ³الحاضر

15 فبهذه الافكار وامثالها كنت ادرس فى الليل والنهار واجرت حياتى

هكذا بغيض لا يوصف وكنت مرارا كتيرة اذهب الى منازل الفلاسفة   Recog. I. 3<br>Hom. I. 3

واسالهم عن هذه الاشيا لاعلم الحق فاقوام منهم قالوا لى بان

النفس غير مايتة وغيرهم قالوا بضد ذلك وغيرهم فقالوا غير ذلك

وكانت نفسى متجلّدة لكى اعرف الحق وايضا كنت اطلب من

20 الحكما لكى اعرف هل يوجد فى تلك الدار عذاب وطرطروس   Recog. I. 4<br>Hom. I. 4

وجهنم النار يُعاقبون فيها الاشرار بعد الموت وهل للصالحين نياحا

---

³ الحاضر .Cod     ² ظلالته .Cod     ¹ اومر .Cod

موبدا لكى استسير بالفضايل فى هذا العالم الحاضر¹ ولا اُعاقب    f. 188 b

هناك دايما وكان عندى وفى قلبى شوقا مثل هذا لا يفتر فسمعت

بان فى بلد اليهودية قد ظهر نبيا عظيما متكامل فى القداسة    Recog. I. 6   Hom. I. 6

ريس اليهود وهو يبشر بملكوت الله ويعلم الشعب خلاصهم ويعمل

5 عجايبا مذهلة لانه ينير العميان وينهض المخلعين ويقيم الاموات

ويعمل جرايحا عظيمة مثل هذه ويكرز بان كل الذين يستسيرون

بالفضايل فى هذا العالم الحاضر¹ يذهبون الى ملكوة السماوات فلما

سمعت انا ذلك فرحت كثيرا وكنت مترجيا بان اعلم ما انا مشتاق

اليه وكان مديح هذا كل يوم يزداد ويثبت الى ان اتى انسان    Hom. I. 7

10 من اورشليم الى رومية لعندنا فوقف فى وسط السوق وقال هكذا

للجمع يا رجال اهل رومية تكونوا تعرفوا بان اليوم ابن الله

يوُجد بالجسد فى اورشليم وهو يوعد كل اولايك الطايعين له

والذين يحفظون وصايا الله والمستسيرين بالفضايل بان يحتقروا

الحاضرات² ليحظوا بالباقيات والحياة الدايمة ويجب ان يعرفون بان

15 الثالوث الاها واحد ويامر لكل الساكنين فى العالم بان لا يظلموا

ذواتهم ويتوبوا كلهم عن خطاياهم لكيلا يُلقوا فى النار التى لا

تطفى ويلبثون فيها بجُملتهم بلا اضمحلال فلما سمعت انا هذه

البشارة الحلوة فرحت جدا وتهللت نفسى وتركت للوقت كل

اضطرابات العالم فوجدت مركبا فدخلت فيه وعزمت بان اذهب    Hom. I. 8

20 الى اورشليم لكى احظى بما انا مشتاق اليه واسمع الحقايق من

فمه فلما سرنا اصابنا هوا مضاددا فتعوقنا ووصلنا الى الاسكندرية

وهناك سالت عنما شرحته اعلاه فسمعت من كثيرين بان جميع

ما قالوه عنه من اجل هذه العجايب وغيرها فهو حقا وكان

¹ Cod. الحاظر      ² Cod. الحاظرات

f. 189 a
Hom. I. 9

وقتيذ هناك واحدا من التلاميذ مكرما اسمه برنابا وكان موقرا
جدا وكان يخبر لساير العُلما بهذه التقويمات فحينيذ ذهبت انا الى
عنده للوقت فوجدته يعلم الشعب بدالة ويقول عن عجايب يسوع
المسيح ليس بعظمه وافتخار لكن بتواضع ومسكنة ويخبرهم بساير
الحقايق وكانوا الفلاسفة يهزون به ويعلمون اقواما ليسالوه عنما لا ٥
حاجة فيه واما هو فكان يعلم من اجل المسيح ويعطيهم اجوبة

Recog. I. 10
Hom. I. 13

فحينيذ انا وخجتهم وخطفت برنابا من الوسط لكيلا يفعلون به
شيا رديا واخذته الى بيتى وسقطت على قدميه متضرعا اليه بان
يخبرنى بامور المسيح باستقصا وانه اخبرنى بُجملة الحقايق
وعزمت بان اذهب معه الى اورشليم لانه فى هذه الايام كان قد ١٠
ازمع بان يوجد هناك فى عيد الفصح بحسب الموافقة التى
عملها مع بقية الرسل فلكن انا كان لى امور ضرورية فما قدرت
بان اذهب معه جملة فلكن اوعدته بانى بعد ايام يسيرة اوجده
هناك وهكذا عملت وذهبت الى اورشليم فوجدته مع بطرس وانهما

Recog. I. 12
Hom. I. 15

فرحا لما نظرونى ثم تفاوضت مع بطرس وسالته بان يحل لى ١٥

Recog. I. 14
Hom. I. 17

كل الشكوك التى كانت عندى من اجل النفس وهل هى مايتة
او غير مايتة وساير ما كان فى عقلى منما وصفته اعلاه
وان الرسول من دفعة واحدة اوضح لى ساير الحقايق
وجاوبنى الكلى الحكمة عن ساير مسايلى واشفى خاطرى باقوال
عجيبة واظهر لى سر الثالوث المقدس وخلقة العالم وتجسد يسوع ٢٠
المسيح وانه الابن والكلمة وان الاموات يقومون فى النهاية

Recog. I. 19

وللصديقين ولخطاة مجازاة وحرصنى لكى انال المعمودية المقدسة
لارتب مع السيد المسيح لكى اقوم واتمجد معه فى الملكوت السماوية
الابدية ولكيلا يكون عندى شك فى الغبطة الدايمة وقال لى من

جملة اقواله هذه بان من الضرورة ان النفس غير مايتة اذ كان الله

طبعه بان عادل وفايق الصلاح لكى يوفى للصديقين من البشر اذا

قاموا بان ويحظى كل واحد منهم بما هو مستحق بحسب عمله

فللصالحين النياح الحسن والسرور الابدى وللاشرار احزانا وعقوبات

5 لا نهاية لها وكل الذين جحدوا هذه ولم يومنون بها فيعتقدون

بان الله ظالم هو اذ يهمل الحسنين العبادة الفضلا الذين اصطبروا

على احزان مختلفة فى هذا العالم وعقوبات لا توصف وتوفيوا

بالموت المر بان لا يجازيهم بالنعيم لاجل اعمالهم الحسنة واما

الملحدين والمتجاوزين الناموس الذين اجازوا ساير حياتهم بالتنعم

10 والافراح وعند نهايتهم ماتوا بموت حسنا فلا يعاقبهم فى الجحيم

لاجل قبيح افعالهم ثم قال لى بعد ذلك بان سيمن الساحر مزمع

ان يرث النار الابدية فلما سمعت انا منه هذه الاقوال تحققت

بان جميع ما خاطبنى به فهو حقا وانى طلبت من القديس لكى

يعمدنى فقال لى بان اصوم واحتمى مدة ثلثة اشهر لكى انطهر

15 من كافة الاوجاع وحينيذ تستحق للمعمودية الالهية وبعد ذلك بايام

سمعت بان بطرس يريد ان يتجادل بمجاهرة مع سيمن الساحر

وسالت انا لواحد من تلاميذ بطرس اسمه اكيلا عن سيمن الساحر

وكيف هو فاجابنى قايلا هذا سيمن له بالجملة فعل الشيطان لانه

يطغى الشعب ويصنع حيلات كانها عجايب حتى ان الحاضرين[1]

20 ينذهلوا منها لانه يدخل فى النار ولا يحترق ويظهر كالنسر طايرا

فى الهوا ويعمل الحجارة خبزا وياكلوها ويصير حية او جديا او

ذهبا ويتحلى بغير ذلك من الاشكال ويفتح ابوابا مغلقة ويحل

---

[1] Cod. الحاظرين

الحديد ويعمله مثل الشمع ويصنع حوايج وانية البيت ويدعهم بان f. 190 a

يمشوا من ذاتهم ويخدمون ساداتهم ويعمل هذا العادم البر غير

ذلك من الاسحار فلما اخبرنى بذلك اكيلا اتى انسان اسمه زكا Recog. II. 19

وقال لبطرس هوذا قد اجتمع ساير الشعب وسيمن جالسا على Hom. III. 29

الكرسى وهو متسلح كالمحارب والكافة ينتظرون بان يسمعون جدالكم 5

فحينيذ اوصانى بطرس لكى اتنحى لاجل انى غير معتمد ليعمل

هو والرسل صلاة مشاعر ليساعدهم الرب لكيلا يسترجع سيمن الجهال

وبدا فى الجدال مع سيمن ساعات عدة ولما غلبه بطرس لم يصبر Hom. III. 58

لكن هرب الى مدينة صور مخزيا وكان هناك يعمل اسحاره فعلم

بطرس بذلك فارسل اكيلا وانا لكى نذهب الى صور ونستفحص 10 Hom. III. 73

عن سيمن ونكتب اليه الجواب فذهبنا ونزلنا فى بيت الكنعانية

فرنيكيس ابنة ايوستيس بحسب ما اوصانا بطرس وانهما قبلونا بفرح Hom. IV. 1

واكرمونا واخبرونا عن سيمن بانه يعمل هناك اسحاره كحسب

عادته حتى احتسبوه العادمون العقل الله وهكذا كتبنا وارسلنا الى

بطرس وانه للوقت اتى فلما سمع سيمن بمجيه هرب الى غير بلد 15 Recog. IV. 3
Hom. VI. 26

ولم يصبر لمجاهرته واقام بطرس الرسول هناك اياما وعمل عجايبا

كثيرة لكى يخلص الناس من ¹ضلالة سيمن وهكذا بمعونة الله

استرجع الاكثرين الى معرفة الله ثم اجتاز من هناك على شط

البحر وذهب الى طرابلس ²وشرطن على طرابلس اسقفا اسمه ماروطى Recog. IV. 1,
VI. 15

ثم خرجنا من هناك لكى نذهب الى انطاكية الشام وارسل بطرس 20 Hom. VIII. 1
Recog. VII. 1

اكيلا ونيقيطا لكى يذهبوا اولا قدامه ولكى لا يكونوا رفقتنا كثيرين Hom. XII. 1

فيشكون فينا الذين ينظرونا من الحنفا وانى انا فرحت كثيرا لما Recog. VII. 4

سكنى معه وكنت مستعدا فى ساير خدمته وانه قال لى اشكر من Hom. XII. 4

حسن خدمتك وتدبيرك ولكن تكون تعرف بانى انا لست احتاج

¹ Cod. ظلالة        ² Sic in Cod.

f. 190 b
Recog. VII. 6
Hom. XII. 6

الى مواكل مختلفة فلكن الى خبز وزيت فقط وبقول فى بعض

الاوقات ولم اقتنى كما ترانى ثواب ثانية لان كل عقلى فى

الخيرات الصالحة التى لاجلها كل خير احتقر من كل نفسى

١ الحاضرات وبالاخرى لانى انا ولدت من اناس ادنيا وقد ربينا

٥ يتامى وفقرا انا واخى اندراوس ولم يكن لنا قنية كثيرة فلاجل

ذلك اعتدت على المسكنة صابرا على الضيقات فى السفر وعلى غير

Recog. VII. 8
Hom. XII. 8

ذلك من شقا الجسد وبعد ما فاوضنى هكذا سالنى عن والدى

ماذا يقال لهم وماذا يدعون وامرنى بان اخبره عن جنسهم واسماوهم

على التحرير وانى خاطبته على الحقيقة بذلك قايلا بان والدى

١٠ يدُعى فافسطس وهو المتقدم فى اهل رومية ولاجل ذلك دفع اليه

قيصر الملك امراة من جنسه تدعى ماطتيديا واولد منها ولدين

توم ودعا اسماوهما فافستينون وفافستينيانون وبعدهم اولدنى انا الا

انى لم اعرف والدتى بالجملة لانها بعد ما ولدتنى بمدة اخيرا

نظرت والدتى مناما كما اخبرنى بذلك ابى بانها اذا لم تذهب مع

Recog. VII. 9

١٥ ولديها التوم الى غير بلد فاننا نموت كلنا وان والدى وضع امى

Hom. XII. 9

مع ولديها فى مركب واعطاهم مال كثير وجوار وعبيد وغير ذلك

من الاشيا الضرورية وارسلهم الى اثينا لكى يتعلمون الاولاد الكتابة

ومسكنى انا عنده فقط ليتسلى بى وبعد سنة ارسل الى والدتى

مع اناسا فضة للنفقة الى اثينا وان اولايك ايضا لم يرجعوا وفى

٢٠ السنة الثالثة ارسل اخرين وانهم عاودوا اليه فى السنة الرابعة وقالوا

Recog. VII. 10

له بانهم لم يجدوا امى ولا اخوتى ورفقتهم وان والدى حزن

Hom. XII. 10

كثيرا وانه وضع مكانه وكلا وتركنى ولرومية والجميع وانحدر

فى مركب طالبا والدتى واخوتى ومن معهم ومن ذلك الوقت

لم يرجع ولم يرسل لنا كتاب بالجملة وانى ظننت بانه

٢٥ من كثرة حزنه عليهم ادركه الموت او اختنق فى البحر

¹ Cod. الحاظرات

f. 191 a
Recog. VII. 11
Hom. XII. 11

والان لى مدة عشرون سنة لم اسمع عنه خبر فلما سمع بطرس ذلك

بدا يبكى كالمترثى وقال للذين هم معنا فى المركب اعلموا يا احباى

بان اذا اصاب المومنين احزان وعقوبات فيصبروا عليها عارفين بان

لاجلها يستوجبون غفران خطاياهم ويحظون بالفرح الابدى لاجل

حزنهم ١الحاضر فلكن الحنفا الاشقيا فيكابدون وهاهنا العقاب وبعد ٥

الموت ايضا يُعاقبون لاجل كفرهم بالعذاب الذى لا نهاية له فلما

Recog. VII. 12
Hom. XII. 12

خاطبنا بهذا بطرس نظرنا قدامنا جزيرة تُدعى ارواد وان اقوام من

اهلها تضرعوا الى بطرس بان يدخل اليها لاجل نياح يسير وانه

اطاعهم وكان ذلك من تدبير الله لكى اجد هناك ولدتى ولما خرجنا

الى الجزيرة ذهب كل واحد الى حيث يريد وان بطرس بهداية الله ١٠

Recog. VII. 13
Hom. XII. 13

طاف طرقات كثيرة فالتفته امراة مسكينة وطلبت منه صدقة فقال

لها لماذا يا امراة لا تعملين بيديكى وتقتاتين من تعبك فلكن

تطلبى طعامك من الغير فاجابته انا بالشكل لى يدين يا سيدى

ولكنهما محلولات ولا فعل لهما ولست اقدر اعمل بهما خدمة

بالكلية ثم بكيت وتنهدت عظيما وان بطرس توجع لها مترثيا لبكاها ١٥

Recog. VII. 15
Hom. XII. 15

وتضرع اليها بان تخبره بمصابها وحزنها فقالت له بانى انا من

جنس عظيم فى رومية وكان لى رجل جليل القدر وثلثة اولاد

ذكور وان اخو زوجى لما نظر حسنى اراد بان يفصحنى بالزنا

وانا فكان لى شوق عظيم الى العفة بما انه شيا مكرم وانى هربت

من بلدى لكى لا يعلم رجلى بهذا الامر فيقتلنى ولاخوه معا ٢٠

Recog. VII. 16
Hom. XII. 16

واكون انا السبب وهكذا انا كذبت على رجلى بانى رايت منام

بان اسافر مع اولادى الاثنين ليلا نموت كلنا وانه ارسلنا الى اثينا

لكى يتعلموا اولادنا الدرس فى الكتب ولما سرنا فى البحر حُدث

علينا فى اخر الليالى اضطراب عظيم فى البحر فانكسر مركبنا

واختنق كل من كان فيه ما خلا انا الشقية الحظ ٢٥

فانى تمسكت بدفة وبها وصلت الى البر وكنت ارتعد وكان

نصفى مايتا ولما صار النهار فتشت على اولادى فلم اجدهم فاتوا

اقوام فلاحين فوجدونى عريانة فكسونى وعزونى وجابونى الى هذه

القرية واخذتنى امراة ارملة فقيرة الى بيتها وكانت فى كل

٥ يوم تعزينى قايلة بان رجلها كان نوتيا وغرق فى البحر وانا فمن

كثرة حزنى وارتعاد يداى كنت اضبط بيدى عصاة ومن هذه

الجهة توسوست وهذه الامراة التى قبلتنى فهى فى امراض عظيمة

وهى ملقاة طريحة فى منزلها لم تقدر ان تتحرك وليس لنا شيا

نعيش منه غير من صدقة يسيرة يعطونا اياها الناس ونحن

١٠ مستسيرين بضيقة عظيمة معا فلما سمع بطرس كلامها عرف بانها

والدتى فسالها قايلا وماذا كان يدعى رجلك وولديكى وما هى

اسماوهم فقالت له اما رجلى فكان يدعى فافسطس واما اولادى فهم

فافستينوس وفافستينيانوس والصغير يُدعى اكليمنطس وتممت خبرها

فقال لها بطرس بهدى الله ايتها الامراة لانك فى هذا اليوم تنظرين

١٥ ولدك واوصاها بان لا تعمل قلقا الى ان نخرج من الجزيرة ثم

مسك بيدها وجابها الى المركب ولما نظرت انا بطرس كيف

يقتاد الامراة تبسمت ولم اعلم العلة فذهبت انا لاستقبله واعمل له

الكرام واضبط يده وان بطرس قال لها هذا هو اكليمنطس وانها

عانقتنى وقبلتنى وهى باكية ولما انا فانى غضبت لاجل انى

٢٠ لم اعلم السبب فقال لى بطرس اترك امك لتمتع فيك فلما

سمعت انا ذلك بكيت وسقطت اقبل قدميها وان كل ¹الحاضرين

تعجبوا منى بانى كيف انا غنى ²ومنطيقى وولد اناس معظمين.

ووالدتى فهى فى فقر هكذا مقداره واننا ارونا بان نذهب

من تلك الجزيرة فقال بطرس لوالدتى لكى تدخل الى

٢٥ المركب لتسير معنا فاجابته اتضرع اليك يا سيدى بان تدعنى

---

¹ الحاظرين .Cod    ² Sic in Cod.

اولا ان اذهب وانال من رفيقتى صفحا لانها قبلتنى من اجل الرب f. 192 a

واعالتنى علــى حسب مقدرتها لما كانت هذه الفقيرة فــى عافيتها

والان فــهى مطروحة مخلعة فتعجب بطرس من حسن عزم والدتى

وامر ¹فاحضروا قدامه المخلعة وانه قال لها هكذا بمسمع الكل ان

كنت انا اكرز بالحق فانهضى معافاة لكى يومنوا هولاى ²الحاضرين 5

بان الله الواحد خلق العلم كله ³فياله مـن عجب للوقت نهضت

المخلعة وصارت معافاة بجملتها وسجدت للطبيب وشكرت من احسانه

كمــا ينبغى فلما نظرت والدتى ذلك العجب تعجبت هــى وساير

²الحاضرين وتضرعت الى بطرس بان يشفيها ايضا وان بطرس وضع

يده عليها فشفيت للوقت فحينيذ شكرت والدتى من الرسول وانى 10

انا دفعت للمتقدم فــى الجزيرة الف درهم مــن الفضة لاجل انهم Recog. VII. 24
Hom. XII. 24

اقتبلوا والدتى عندهم وامرته بان يفرقها صدقة لاجل محبتى على

الفقرا والمستحقين واننا سرنا مـع والدتى بعد الذى عمد بطرس

الامراة التى اقتبلتها وغيرها وكل الذين امنوا بتعليم الرسول وذهبنا

من هناك طايفين من بلد الى غيره الى ان بلغنا الى لالاذقية 15 Recog. VII. 25
Hom. XIII. 1

وهناك استقبلونا اكيلا ونيقيطا وقبلونا كــما ينبغى لضايفين الغربا

وان بطرس لما نظر عظم تلك المدينة وكثرة اهلها عزم بان يقيم

هناك اياما كثيرة لكى يكرز بقول الايمان وحينيذ نيقيطا واكيلا

سالونى من اجل والدتى قايلين من هى هذه الامراة ومن اين

رافقتكم وان بطرس اخبرهم بقصتها من اولها الى اخرها فلما سمعا قوله 20 Recog. VII. 26, 27
Hom. XIII. 2
Recog. VII. 28

لبثا منذهلين ساعات عدة وبعد ذلك صرخا هكذا بدموع قايلين نحن

هم اولادها فافستينوس وفافستينيانوس اخوة اكليمنظس ثم انهما اخبرا Hom. XIII. 3

قدام والدتهما بكلما جرى عليهما مع النوتية قايلين بان انكسر مركبنا Recog. VII. 32

¹ Cod. فااحظروا     ² Cod. الحاظرين     ³ Sic in Cod.

f. 192 b
Hom. XIII. 7

وللوقت كان بقربنا مركب فيه لصوص البحر فاخذونا معهم فى

مركبهم وذهبوا بنا الى قيسارية فيلبس وغيروا اسامينا وباعونا فاشترتنا

امراة عالمة وغنية جدا تسمى ايوسطا واحبتنا كمثل اولادها الخصيصين

وادبتنا بكافة علوم اليونانيين ولما كبرنا اتعلمنا ايضا الفلسفة لكى

5 نوعظ ونعلم الامم لكى نقتادهم الى الامانة الحسنة وكنا مشتاقين

Recog. VII. 33

بان نتعلم غش الاصنام والباطلات وبعد هذا اتفقنا مع انسان يدعى

Hom. XIII. 8

سيمن لانه توهم بان يطغينا على حسب عزمه النجس فلكن من

فعل الله اصطحبنا مع واحد من تلاميذ المسيح يدعى زكا وانه

علمنا بان نترك سيمن واقتادنا الى رسول الرب بطرس وانه وعظنا

10 وعمدنا وهكذا نحن نطلب من الله بان يوهلك وانت للمعمودية

المقدسة فلما اخبرا بهذا عانقا والدتى يبكون بدموع غزيرة وابتهاج

Recog. VII. 34

وحينيذ طلبت انا من الرسول بطرس بان انال المعمودية المقدسة

وانه اوصانى بان اصوم ايضا مدة ايام مجاهدين بالصوم واننا تضرعنا

اليه لكى يعمدنا لانا كنا من حين دخلنا الى المركب لم ناكل

15 شيا وهكذا شهدت والدتى وتضرعنا ايضا لكى يعمدنا لناكل معها

خبزا لنفرح بالروح لانى انا غير معتمد ولم ناكل فى مايدة

واحدة بالجُملة وان بطرس لكيلا يخطى قدام الله بما انه قديس

Recog. VII. 37

ولكى يعمل ايضا شهوتنا امرنا بان نصوم كل ذلك اليوم معه وفى

اليوم المقبل لكى نستحق للمعمودية المقدسة وهكذا صنع وبعد

Hom. XIV. 1

20 عمادنا اتناول بطرس خبزا وبارك وقدس الخبز وكسره وناوله لوالدتى

اولا ونحن بعد ذلك واكلنا فرحين وممجدين لله ومن بعد ذلك اتانا

Recog. VIII. 1
Hom. XIV. 2

واحد شيخ وقال هكذا لبطرس لا تطغى يا انسان ولا تصلى فان ليس

Recog. VIII. 2

لله وجود ولا تدبير اله فلكن نصيب كل انسان فقط وكلما هو مزمع

بان يصيب الانسان خيرا او شرا يحظى به ان صلَّى واذا لم   f. 193 a
Hom. XIV. 3

يصلَّى كما اعرف انا عملى لانى انا كنت موسرا جدا وذو حسب

وكنت اجود على الفقرا بصدقات كثيرة لكى يعينونى الالهة ولكيلا

يصيبنى حزن من احد من الاشيا المزمعة ان تجرَّى علي فلكن لم

يقتدروا الالهة بان يحفظونى بغير مصاب هذه واكثر منها قالـها   5

الشيخ لبطرس واما بطرس فكان يعاند قوله واظهر له الحق قايلا

بانه قد يوجد الاها واحدا فقط وهو غير مايت وهو الذى سبق

ودبر كافة الاشيا بحكمته العادلة وبعضها بمسامحة منه وبعد ذلك

ساله بطرس بان يقول له من اين هو وماذا اصابه وجرى عليه

من البلايا فاجابه قايلا انا كنت من اكابر رومية عارفا بصناعة   10

التنجيم جدا وكنت متزوج بامراة قد كانت من جنس قيصر

الملك واولدت منها ثلثة اولاد وكان مكتوب لها فى حظها بان   Recog. IX. 32

تصير فاسقة لانها احبت واحد من عبيدها ولما لم تقدر ان تصبر   Hom. XIV. 6

علـى دينونة الناس لها فهربت معه الى غير بلـد واخذت معها   Hom. XIV. 7

الولدين الكبار وابقت الولد الصغير عندى واتزوجت هى بذلك العبد   15

وهكذا ماتت مع ولديها واما ابنى الصغير فلبث فى بيتى واخيرا

ذهبت انا لاطلب الامراة وولديها فضاع ايضا ابنى الصغير وها انا

دايرا من مكـان الى مكان ولست اقدر اعاود الى موطنى لاجل

خجلـى وانا الان بتعب عظيم وعذاب احصّل طعامى فلما سمع

بطرس ذلك عرف بان الشيخ هو والدى بالحقيقة وساله عن اسمه   20   Hom. XIV. 8

وعن اسم زوجته واولاده فاجابه بان اسمـى فافسطس وزوجتى

ماطتيديا واولادى فافستينوس وفافستينيانوس والصغير كليمنس فحينيذ

بكيت انا وبطرس وعند ذلك ذهبت الى عند امى وبشرتها   Hom. XIV. 9

بانى وجدت والدى رجلها وانها خرجت وهى تصرخ وتبكى وتفتش

عليه فلما عرفته فمن كثرة فرحها اقامت ساعات كثيرة صامتة

كالميت ثم ¹حضرنا نحن الاولاد الثلثة وسجدنا لابينا وقلنا له باننا

نحن اولادك وصار لنا كلنا فى ذلك اليوم فرحا لا يوصف وشكرنا

5 الله القادر على كل شى الذى اهلنا بان يتمتع احدنا بالاخر وبعد

ذلك اتجادل بطرس مع ابى ووعظه لكى يومن بالمسيح وانهاه بان

لا يقول ذلك الهذيان الذى قاله اولا ولكى يومن بان الله حقا

هو وبكلية حكمته سبق ودبّر بان تجرى عليكم هذه المصايب وينكسر

المركب ويفترق احدكم من الاخر لكى بعد هذه الاحزان التى

10 دهمتكم تجتمعوا ايضا وتستنيروا بالامانة الحقيقية واخر الكل بوعظ

كثير وتعليم واضح عرف والدى الحق وتقدم الى حسن العبادة

ولما امن بالمسيح واعتمد ²فامتلى غيرةً الاهية واخذ من بطرس

صفحا وذهب ليتجادل مع سيمن الساحر لانه كان وقتيذ فى

انطاكية ولما نظر سيمن بان والدى قد وجه قدام الشعب كمثل

15 وساحر اعتاض العادم البر وبدا يتشكل ويظهر حيلاته الشيطانية وان

والدى ايضا بدا يتشكل ويتصنع ويعمل ذاته كانه سيمن الساحر

ثم ان الكافر سيمن عمل شكله مثل شكل والدى لاجل ان الملك

كان قد ارسل اجناد من رومية ليمسكوا سيمن ويجيبوه مربوطا

الى رومية بما انه ³ضالل وساحر ويقتلوه كحسب استحقاقه وان

20 الغاش لكى يهرب من هذه الشدة تشكل بصورة ابى لكى يقتلوه

عوض سيمن واما سيمن فانه هرب الى بلد اليهودية وصار غايبا

ثم بعد ذلك لما اتى والدنا من انطاكية الى عندنا فنظرناه

كمثل سيمن فتعجبنا ثم ان بطرس سمع من الانطاكيين

بان سيمن قد علّم كل اهل انطاكية طغيانه وحركهم لكى

يقتلوا الرسول بطرس اذا ذهب الى عندهم كمثل ضالل وطاغى ‹ f. 194 a

وهم الان كلهم مستعدين لكى يتمموا قول سيمن فلما سمع بطرس

ذلك ارسل والدى مع اخوتى الاثنين ووالدتى واقوام غيرهم لكى

يذهبوا الى انطاكية قايلا لوالدى اذهب يا فافسطس الان الى Recog. x. 60
Hom. xx. 18, 19

انطاكية واظهر صورة سيمن واكرز للشعب كمن فمه لكى يعرفوا 5

الحق ويومنوا بان الله واحدا هو على الحقيقة وابدى وما شابه

ذلك وان والدى ذهب الى انطاكية بفرح كحسب وصية بطرس

له وانتصب فى وسط المدينة وهتف هكذا لتكونوا تعرفوا يا اهل

انطاكية باننا قد ظلمنا بطرس لما قرفناه لان ذلك الانسان قديسا Recog. x. 66

وانا فقد تجنيت عليه بالباطل فلكن الان اتضرع اليكم بان تقبلوه 10

اذا جا وتومنوا وتصدقوا بتعليمه لاجل انه رسول الله الحقيقى

الغير كاذب واعملوا جميع ما يامركم به واذا لم تعملون هكذا

به فانه يهلككم كلكم ولمدينتكم معا وانا لاجل هذا الامر اتيت

الى عندكم لاعطيكم خبر لكيلا تصنعون به شرا لانى انا فى الليلة

الماضية ظهروا لى ملايكة وضربونى كمثل كافر وباغض الانذار 15

بالحق فاتضرع اليكم بهذا واعلموا ايضا بانى انا قد كنت جيت الى

عندكم غير دفعة واطغيتكم من فعل الشيطان وتكلمت على بطرس

قولا رديا فلا تصدقونى وانا اليوم اعترف قدامكم بمجاهرة بانى

انا طاغى وساحر فلكنى الان قد رجعت الى التوبة مترجيا بان الله

يغفر خطاياى فلما قال هكذا والدى للانطاكيين عن وجه سيمن 20

وبارك بطرس ومدحه فللوقت احال عزم كل الانطاكيين الذين كانوا

يبغضوا الرسول قديما وجعلهم ان يحبوه وان والدى ارسل الينا خبر

بان نذهب الى هناك لكى يتمتع بحلاوة وعظ بطرس وانى انا للوقت

ذهبت مع بطرس وساير رفقتنا وان كل الانطاكيين قبلوه بفرح Recog. x. 68
Hom. xx. 23

¹ Cod. ظالل

عظيم بما انه نذيرا بالحق ورسولا لله وكـان يصلى ويضع يده

اليمين على المرضى ويشفيهم كلهم وعلّم شعبا جزيلا بان يومنوا

بالاله المثلث بالاقانيم ووطد الامانة الحسنة ثم ان ابى سقط على

قدمى بطرس متضرعا اليه لكى يعمله مسيحيا ويتممه بالمعمودية

5 المقدسة لكى يرجع الى صورته الاولة ويتناول الاسرار الالهية وان

بطرس اوصاه بان يبكى ويصوم الى الغد وفى اليوم الثانى وعظه

ولكثيرين غيره جدا وعلمهم بان يستسيروا بالامانة المستقيمة بلا عيب

وعمدهم بسم الاب والابن وروح القدس وبعد ذلك اقام هناك اياما

كثيرة يعلم الانطاكيين وقاسينا كلنا شدايدا كثيرة من الشيطان

10 عدو الحق ولما سمع الوالى باننا نحن من جنس قيصر الملك فارسل

اخبر الملك طيباريوس بذلك وان الملك لما علم بهذا ارسل يقول

له بان يرسل والدى ووالدتى الى رومية سريعا وان الوالى منحهم

عطايا عظيمة واكرمهم كثيرا وارسلهم وان الملك لما نظر والدى

ووالدتى بكى كثيرا من زيادة ابتهاجه ووقع على اعناقهما مقابلا

15 ايهما وقال هكذا لساير اراكنته افرحوا اليوم كلكم معى وهلموا

لنعمل عيدا مشاعا لوجودنا فافسطس وماطتيديان لاننا توهمناهم

اموات فقاموا ¹وضاليـن ووجدوا وعمل لـهم مايدة عظيمة واكل

معهم ثم اوهبهم ذهبا كثيرا وعبيدا وجوارا وغير ذلك من المواهب

الجليلة لاجل شرف جنسهم ليستسيروا كحسب عادتهم الاولة

20 وانهما اتعرفا فى رومية بالفضايل وحسن العبادة ²حايطين امانة

المسيح غير منزعزعة واخيرا قسموا على المساكين ساير متاعهم

واتقنوا كافة الصالحات واكملا حياتهما فيما يرضى اللـه

وتركا ¹الحاضرات وورثوا السماويات فاما انا واخوتى فاننا لم f. 195 a
ننفصل من معلمنا بطرس بالجُملة فلكن كنا معه دايما فى طاعته
واسفاره واحتملنا معه كل احزان وعقوبات مختالفة اصطبرنا عليها
من الكفار الذين فى المُدن والقرى لما ذهبنا لنكرز بالانجيل
وفى الاخر انتهينا الى رومية المشهورة واكرز فيها بطرس بمجاهرة 5
بالمسيح وصنع عجايبا كثيرة واسترجع كثيرين الى الامانة وعمدهم
وليس من الادنيا فقط فلكن اغنيا كثيرين ونسوة من بيت
الملك الذين كانت منهم مطرونة الحسيبة الا ان الرسول بطرس
لما ازمع بان يذهب الى عند المسيح معلّمنا ابصر منظرا الاهيا
بانه بعد ايام يسيرة يريد يُصلب لكى يصير شريكا لالام سيده 10
وانه جمع كل الاخوة وانتصب فى وسط الكنيسة وضبط يدى
وقال هكذا للجمع تكونوا تعرفوا هذا يا اخوتى واولادى بانى قد
وصلت الى نهاية حياتى بحسبما اظهر لى سيدى المسيح وهوذا
انا اشرطن عليكم هذا تلميذى اكليمنظس اسقفا وهو الذى
اوثقته على كرسى راعيا لكم من اليوم لانه شاركنى فى كل 15
امتحاناتى واحزانى الذى صابرناها وانا عارفا به بانه عابد الله
المحب البشر ونقيا وعفيفا وصالحا وصديقا وطويل الاناة ويصبر
على الاحزان وساير الاشيا المضاددة التى توافى اليه ولاجل هذا
امنحه سلطان لكى يحل ويربط كلما ينبغى لانه عارفا بقوانين
الكنيسة جيدا جدا فيجب عليكم كلكم بان تخضعوا له 20
لان كلمن يمرمر الريس الحقانى فانه يسخط الله ويرث موت
المخالفين وعقوباتهم ويجب ايضا على المتقدم بان يشابه
الطبيب الحقانى ولا يتسخط بعدم معرفة فلما قال

¹ Cod. الحاظرات.

بطرس هكذا سقطت انا على قدامه معتفيا من الرياسة وانه

قال لى لا تضادد يا ابنى مشية الله والتفت نحو الشعب واوصاهم

كلهم لكى يستسيروا بالامانة بكل طهارة وبغير عيب وان يهب

احدهم للاخر وان عرض لاحدهم مع الاخر شكًّا او قلقا فيعمل

5 معه محبة قبل ان تغيب الشمس ولا يدينوا احد ولكن يصفحوا

لمن اخطى اليهم لكى الله يغفر ويصفح لهم عن خطاياهم

ثم اوصى لجميعهم ايضا بان يكون لهم في انا ورعا عظيما كمثل

الورع الذى كان لهم فيه فلما وعظهم بهذه المواعظ واكثر منها

جلس فى الكرسى وقال لى اتضرع اليك بان تكتب الى يعقوب اخا

10 الرب بعد مماتى وخروجى من الحياة كل الذى جرى عليك

منذ صغر سنك وماذا صار علينا فى اسفارنا الى اليوم وانصرافى انا

وكمال شهادتى وكيف امجد الله بموتى مصلوبا كما فاوضنى

الرب لانه اذا سمع هذا يريد يناله سرورا عظيما وسلوة واما انا

اكليمنظس فلكى اخالف وصية معلمى بطرس كتبت اليك يا

15 سيدى يعقوب وارسلت اليك باختصار كل ذلك الذى جرى علىّ

وصلّى انت من اجلى الى الرب لكى يوهلنى انا الغير مستحق

بان ارعى ما قد اثمنت عليه رعاية مرضية لله وان اثمر حياتى بالشهادة


<br>

خبر شهادة القديس اكليمنظس


الى هاهنا هى رسالة هذا المغبوط اكليمنظس التى كتبها بيده

20 الى الرسول يعقوب التى منها يقدر بان يفهم كل احد كثرة

محبته للرب وغيرته للامانة الحسنة لكى بالاكثر يعرف من نهاية هذا

المغبوط بالشهادة لانه اصطبر عليها المثلث الغبطة بشهامة لكى يمجد

الرب ويشدد الامانة الحسنة بها انه تلميذا حسنا لبطرس ومستحقا

f. 196 a لخلافة كرسيه لانه شابه معلمه فى الفضايل بالعادات الحسنة

والجهادات وباقى الفضايل وكان معلما لليهود والحنفا وصار مع

الكل كالكل لكيما يربح الكافة لينتصبوا فى حسن العبادة للمسيح

وكان متواضعا جدا حلوا فى خطابه ووعظه حتى ان اليونانيين

واليهود كان لهم فيه محبة عظيمة وورعا لاجل انه لم يكن ٥

يوجح بانتهار وتوحش ولكن بتواضع كثير ووداعة موضحا لهم

الشهادات من كتبهم ليكون قوله مستحقا لتصديقه ولم يكن يشتم

احد منهم ولا يرفضهم بالجملة وكان يوضح للعادمين العقل عن

اصنامهم واحدا فواحدا كيف كانوا ومن هم ويوضح لهم حقريتهم

ولاجل اى علّم توهّموهم الهة وكان فى اخر وعظه يكرز دايما ١٠

بكثرة تحنن اللـه الحقيقى وغزارة رحمته ويحركهم الى التوبة

ويوعدهم بان ملكوة السما مفتوحة للراجعين منهم وذلك بان يكفوا

عن خطاياهم الاولة فقط ويومنوا بالمسيح ويعتمدوا فان الله يقبلهم

واما اليهود فكان يمدحهم فى اول كلامه قايلا بانهم شعبا لله

مُنتخبا بما انهم من .جنس ابرهيم وما شابه ذلك من المدايح وفى ١٥

الاخر فكان يكرم العهد الجديد ولا يحتقر العتيقة حتى لا يشكون

فلكن كان يتمم قوله بالحكمة وهكذا عمل مع كثيرين منافعا

كثيرة مهتديا بكلامه ومقتاد كل احد الى حسن العباده وكان

ايضا مهتما بتدبير المسيحيين دايما معتنق امـور المساكين لكيلا

يعوزهم شيا مـن ضروريات الجسد الذين هم مـن الرجال والنسا ٢٠

الارامـل واليتامى الذيـن فى المدينة وكتبهم كلهم فى دفتر

وكان يعطى لكل احد منهم صدقة بقدر ما ينبغى لكى

يـدبّر معيشته فـهكذا عمـل المتحنن اكليمنظس المشابه برحمة

للمسيح وكانوا سايـر حاشية الملك يكرموه ويوقروه مـا خلا

واحدا منهم اسمه سيسينيوس كان يخبر نارن الملك كثيرا فهذا

كان يبغضه واخبر للملك عن ذاته بان اكليمنظس استرجع

زوجته ثاودرة من عبادة الاصنام وانها ليس هي الان مهتمة فى

بيتها واولادها لكن فى كل وقت تذهب الى كنيسة المسيحيين

5 لتتعلم تعاليمهم وكانت هذه البغضة فى قلب سيسينيوس وكان

متسلحا فى كل يوم بسلاح الظلم والغيرة والحسد المكمن فى

قلبه على القديس وكان يدرس على زوجته ثاودرة بالسو اذا وجد

وقتا موافقا وفى بعض الايام تخابث وكان مجمع المسيحيين

وانه ذهب واختفى فى الكنيسة مع عبيده لينظر ماذا تفعل زوجته

10 هناك وعند حصوله فى الكنيسة فكان القديس وقتيذ يصلى فللوقت

لبث سيسينيوس [1]اعما واطرشا وانه قال لعبيده خذونى واقتادونى

لكى اذهب الى بيتى لانه قد دهمنى العما والطرش على غفلة

وهوذا لست انظر ولا اسمع بالجملة وان العبيد اقتادوه بيده وارادوا

بان يخرجوا فيه من الكنيسة فلم يقدروا فلكن كانوا يدوروا

15 هاهنا وهناك بغير منفعة لان القوة الالهية منعتهم ليتادّب ذلك العديم

العقل ويتعنّف وان ثاودرة لما نظرته هكذا سالت عن علته

فاخبروها بامره وانها تضرعت الى الرب بدموع لكى يسمح له

بالخروج وهكذا صار فجابوه عبيده الى بيته ووضعوه فى الفراش

وهو اعمى واطرش بفعل الله فلما رجعت ثاودرة الى بيتها

20 فاخبروها بامره على الاستقصا وانها حزنت وتربدت له وذهبت

ووقعت على قدمى القديس وهى متضرّعة بدموع لكى يشفى

رجلها وان اكليمنظس ذهب الى بيت المريض ويبكى عليه

وتضرع الى الله مصليا من اجله وقايلا ايها الرب يسوع

المسيح يا من اعطيت مفاتيح ملكوتك لرسولك بطرس

---

[1] Sic in Cod.

لكى يفتح ويغلق لمن يريد فانت افتح عينى واذنى هذا الرجل f. 197 a
لانك اوعدتنا بان تعطينا بصلاحك ساير مطلوباتنا فلما صلّى
القديس هكذا من اجل المريض فللوقت شفى من عماه الحسى
وسمع باذنيه الحسية فلكن نفسه لبث ايضا فى ¹الضلالة القديمة
وكان يتوهم بان القديس ساحر ويعمل هذه الاشيا باسحاره وعمية 5
بصيرة الشقى كمثل الاول ²بالضلالة وان الغير شكور اوصا خدامه
بان يمسكوا القديس وقتيذ ويربطوه ليجازيه عوض النعمة بضدها
وان الخدام مسكوا خشبا وحجارة ظانين بانهم القديس وربطوهم
لانهم توسوسوا من المجازاة الالهية وان سيسينيوس توهم بان
عبيده قد ربطوا القديس فافتخر عليه قايلا له هكذا انا ابطل يا 10
اكليمنظس اسحارك وطغيانك سريعا لكى تتادب وان القديس كان
محفوظا بغير رباط وتقدم وقال له هكذا يا عديم العقل لقد
عمى فلبك ايها الشقى فلا تتوهّم بان تربطنى انا فلكن اربط
الهتك الذين تسجد لهم منذ الاول وتركه محتقرا مرذولا ثم ان
القديس بارك ثاودورة واوصاها لكى تصلّى الى الله بغير فتور من 15
اجل رجلها لكى يرجع الى حسن العبادة وانها كانت تصلّى
متضرعة الى الله بدموع من اجله فظهر لها عند المسا انسان
لحيته بيضا موقرا بشبه بطرس الرسول وقال لها لاجلك اشفيت
رجلك لكيما يتقدس الرجل من الامراة كما اوصى اخى بولص
الرسول ولما قال لها هكذا غاب للوقت وان سيسينيوس بفعل 20
النعمة الالهية دعا زوجته وقال لها انا قد امنت بسيدى
يسوع المسيح الاله الحقيقى وحده الذى تضرعت اليه انا
ليغفر لى جهالاتى القديمة وثانيا فانتى اتشفعى لى عند القديس
اكليمنظس بان لا يحقد علّي انا الغير شكور وبما انه تلميذ لله

بالظلالة Cod. ²      الظلالة Cod. ¹

f. 197 b

يتحنن علـي وان الامراة لمـا سمعت ذلك فرحت وبكيت وانها

للوقت اخبرت البار بذلك فاسرع للوقت وجا الى بيت سيسينيوس

وانه اقتبله بتواضع كثير وسقط على قدميه باكيا بحرارة وقال له

بقلب منسحق اشكر الاله الحقيقى ولقدسك لانك اعميت حدقتى

٥　الحسيات¹ وانرت نفسى لكى اعرف الحق واهرب من ²ضلالة اليونانيين

وكذبهم لانى مـن كـل قلبى اقتبلت الانذار بالامانة الحسنة

وكان حينيذ عيد الفصح فصار وقتيذ فى ذلك البيت عيدا عظيما

وعمد سيسينيوس وكل اهله ومحبيه وعبيده مـن الرجال والنسا

وكانت عدتهم اربعماية وثلثة وعشرون انسان وكان منهم اقواما

١٠　كثيرين مـن محبى الملك ومعارفه فلما عاين ذلك بوبليوس

القويص الكلى شره بان الامانة وقتيذ تنمو وتزيد وضع فى عقله

بان يقتل القديس الذى هو علة هذه الاشيا وانه دفع الى اقوام فضة

وتوافق معهم بـان يعملون سجس مع والى المدينة ويقرفوا القديس

قدامه ليحركوه على قتلة سريعا فاتوا هولاى للوالى وقرفوا القديس

١٥　بانه ³مضل وساحر وانه يجدف علـى الالهة وقلع هياكلهم من

الاساسات ويسجد لاله جديد وابتنى له فى كل مكان كنايس

ومذابح ثم ان الذين لم ياخذوا رشوة مدحوا القديس قدام الوالى

مخبرين بعجايبه والاحسانات التى يفعلها مع كل المدينة فلما

انظر الوالى كثرة محاورة الشعب وقلقهم دعا للقديس فى السر

٢٠　وامتحنه بتمليقات كثيرة لكى يرجع الى ²ضلالته ولما راه جلدا

شهما وغير متقلقلا اورد خبره قدام طراييانوس الملك قايلا له بان

سجسا عظيما صايرا فى المدينة من اجل اكليمنظس وان الملك

حتم عليه بان ينفوه الى مدينة مقفرة هى فى حدود شرصونة وان

الوالى حزن على القديس لاجل انه مزمع ان يذهب الى هذا المنفى

¹ Sic in Cod.　　² Cod. ظلالته　　³ Cod. مظل

A. P.

9

الممر وانه استحضره وامره بان يضحى للاصنام ولا يذهب الى هذا

المنفى وان القديس اراد بعذوبة الفاظه وحلاوتها بـان يسترجع

الوالى الى الايمان بالمسيح فلما نظر الوالى عدم انقياد القديس

ودعه وهو متنهدا وباكيا قايلا له الله الذى تعبده هو يعينك على

هذا المنفى الصعب ثمر انه اعدّ له ساير حوايجه وارسله فى مركب ٥

وعانقه وقبله واطلقه فاتبعوه كثيرين مـن الورعين الـى المنفى

ووجد هناك عدة الفين من المسيحيين المظلومين المنفيين سابقا

وكانوا يقطعون هناك مومرا وانهمر لما نظروا القديس فرحوا جدا

وسجدوا لـه وقبلوا اياديه بورع واخبروه بمصابهمر وضيقتهمر وعدمهمر

حتى وللشى الضرورى واشر من هذا كله فليس كان عندهمر مـا ١٠

لاجل عملهمر وتعبهمر وكثرة شقاهمر لكى يندى عطشهمر فلكن كانـوا

يذهبون ويجيبون الما مـن مكـان بعيد مقداره خمسة واربعين

غلوة فتوجع القديس لاجلهمر باكيا ثمر عزاهمر كثيرا قايلا لهمر بان

مشية الله كانت بان ننفى ونتشارك فى العقوبات والالامر فلما قال

هكذا اوصاهمر بان يعملوا جميعهمر صلاة مشاعر معه متضرعين الى ١٥

الله القادر على كل شى لكى يعطيهمر ما بما انه متحنن وعند

ما اكمل القديس صلاته نظر الى هاهنا وهنا وانه نظر من بعيد

خروفا يرفع رجله اليمين ويوضح الارض التى قدامه والخروف فلمر

ينظره احدا غير القديس وانه ذهب مع ثلثة اناس وقال لهمر حفروا

هذا المـكـان الذى كـان واقفا فيه الخروف فلمـا عملوا حفرة ٢٠

صغيرة اتناول البار الفاس بيده وحفر به يسيرا وقال هكذا بسمر سيدنا

يسوع المسيح يخرج فى هذا الموضع مـا حلوا عذبا فلما قال

هـكـذا يا لعجايبك ايها المسيح الملك القادر علـى كـل شى

فللوقت خرج ما غزيرا هناك وصار نهرا عظيما وكان ما حلوا

لذيذا فاتناول القديس منها وشرب وكذلك كلهم شربوا فرحين ومن

اجل هذا العجب اكرموا اهل القرى الذين هناك للقديس وتورعوه

وكانوا يتبادروا اليه فى كل وقت وكانوا يسمعوا حلاوة تعليمه

5 واسترجع منهم اقواما لا يُحصون الى حسن العبادة وعمدهم بسم

الثالوث المقدس وهدم هياكل الاصنام وابتنى لهم كنايس لانه فى

مدة سنة من مقامه هناك ابتنى القديس للذين امنوا خمسة وسبعين

كنيسة واحرق واتلف ساير الاصنام واباد ساير اثاراتهم فلما علم

الملك ارسل الى افيديانون الوالى بان يحرص بكل وجه لكى

10 يبطل امانة المسيح وان الوالى عاقب هناك كثيرا من المسيحيين

باصناف التعاذيب فلما نظر بان الجميع مشتاقين لكى يستشهدوا

لاجل المسيح وهم مستعدين لذلك وضع فى عقله بان يقتل

القديس الذى هو علة ذلك وانه اوقع بالمغبوط اكليمنظس

التعاذيب الصعبة وعاقبه كثيرا فلما نظره بانه مشتاق الى الشهادة

15 بزيادة وهو يشدد المومنين ويوطدهم حكم عليه بالقتل وان يربطوا

فى عنقه حبل المركب الغليظ ويطرحوه فى عُمق البحر لكيلا

يجدوا المومنين جسده المكرم فلما اطرحوه فى البحر وقف جمعا

جزيلا من المسيحيين بقرب البحر وهم نايحين وباكيين على

معلمهم وان كرنيليوس وفيفس تلميديه صرخا بحزن لا عزا له

20 وامروا البقية بان يصلوا الى الله كلهم مشاعا متضرعين اليه

بان يخرج جسد القديس الى الارض فلما صلوا كلهم معا

وهم باكيين صار عجبا عظيما لان فى بعض الاوقات اكمل

موسى فى البحر الاحمر عجبا مذهلا وهاهنا صار وكمل عجبا

معجزا وذلك بان البحر هرب الى خلف عشرون ميلا وتقدموا

المسيحيين على البر ١فيلافراط قوتك ايها المسيح القادر على
كل شى فوجدوا حجرا عظيما منحوتا مثل الكنيسة ومهندما بصناعة
عجيبة بحكمة الله المذهلة وفى وسطه هيكلا بهيا وهناك جسد
القديس المكرم موضوعا منيرا وبقرب ذلك الحجر العظيم الثقيل
ذلك الحبل الجافى المذكور فاراد كرنيليوس وفيفس بان يرفعا ٥
القديس فسمعا صوتا سماويا يقول لهر هكذا اتركوه حيث الرب
العجيب دفنه فتركوه وبتلك القوة فهو الى الان فى كل سنة
لاكرام وتذكار الشاهد فيرجع البحر الى خلف فى يوم تذكار
القديس ويقف هكذا مدة سبعة ايام لكى ياتوا المومنين ويعيدوا
لموسمه المقدس فلما سمعوا الجمع ذلك الصوت مجدوا الله وقبلوا ١٠
جسد القديس فقط ورجعوا وهم فرحين وليس فى ذلك الوقت صار
هذا العجب فقط وغيره من العجايب المذهلة لكن وفى كل سنة
فى تذكار هذا القديس يهرب البحر الى خلف كما ذكرنا ويعطى
للناس وقتا لكى يعيدوا الموسم القديس وصار وقتيذ عجايبا غير هذه
كثيرة لان كل الذين يذهبون الى هناك ويكونوا بسو حال من ١٥
الامراض ويشربون من ما ذلك البحر بحيث هيكل هذا القديس
فيبرون من كافة اسقامهم وبعد ايام يسيرة فصاروا كل الذين
يسكنون بقرب ذلك المكان مسيحيين لما عاينوا هذه العجايب
المذهلة فلكن اسمعوا عجيبة اعظم من كل هذه العجايب وذلك
بانه كان انسان مومن وله امانة عظيمة فى هذا القديس فذهب ٢٠
ليسجد للقديس فى هيكله هذا المذكور مع زوجته ورفقته وكان
له ابن صغير وانهر لما قرب رجوعهر وقفوا فى هيكل هذا القديس
يصلون ليمنح الله ولدهر حياة مديدة وغير ذلك ولما ازمع البحر
بان يرجع الى مكانه هربوا والدين الصبى مع غيرهم من
المسيحيين بحرص شديد لكيلا يغطيهر البحر ومن الخوف والقلق ٢٥

الكثير تركوا هناك الصبى ولم يفطنو بان ما البحر يغطيه كالقبر

وحينيذ لما فتشوا عليه ولم يجدوه عرفوا بانه لبث فى هيكل القديس

وانهم بكيوا عليه شديدا ورجعوا الى منزلهم ولما نظروا ثيابه ايضا

ازداد انتحابهم عليه وكانوا لا سلوة لهم فلما عبرت تلك السنة

5 ووافى عيد هذا القديس فذهبوا هولاى ليفتشوا لعلهم يجدون عظام

ولدهم فلما رجع البحر كعادته فى كل سنة الى خلف فتبادروا

هولاى قدام الكل الى هيكل الشاهد فلما وصلوا الى هناك وجدوا

ولدهم وهو واقفا بقربة قبر القديس فاولا شكوا به وظنوا خيلا ولما

نظروه جيدا وتحققوا بانه ولدهم فاحتضنوه وقبلوه ومن كثرة فرحهم

10 بكيوا وسالوه من اين كنت تاكل فى هذه السنة وكيف انحفظت

من حيتان البحر بغير ضرر وان الولد اومى باصبعه الى القديس

وقال هذا كان يعولنى ويحفظنى وحينيذ رجع حزن والديه الى

فرح وشكروا الله قايلين عجيبا هو الله فى قديسيه وما شابه ذلك

من التمجيد لله ولما اكملوا العيد رجعوا الى منزلهم فرحين

15 مسرورين ممجدين الله الذى يصنع مشيته 'خايفية ويكرمهم وكانت

شهادة هذا القديس فى اليوم الرابع والعشرون من تشرين الثانى

فنحن نسال الرب الاهنا بان يرزقنا شفاعته ويحصينا معه فى

ملكوة السماوات امين كتبه الفقير ماكاريوس الانطاكى بيده

الفانية واخرجه من اللغة الرومية الى اللغة العربية فى سنة

20 سبعة الاف وماية وسبعة وستين للعالم الموافق الف وستماية

وتسعة وخمسين لتجسد المسيح فى الثانى والعشرون من

كانون الاول وكانت كتابته فى مدينة سُناب المحروسة

ما راد طوسوس يوم الميلاد المحبل
بعد العدا ن في جنة دعسير
توقا مصره ده دانون الاول
٢ سنة ما به دبلده وعا بين
من سنن العرب والله القسم
ابدا فنحن نسل رسا وحلظنا
لیسوع المسیح أن برحمنا بطلوات
عبد السا هد الشريف ابطوس
دار لحمل ها معه في ملل السحط
ونصت ولعف لحا عتنا الجمع
امین استقاعه سدنا هولمس بعر
ام النور امین
لمح
فیه له

قال يوحنا فهم الذهب
املحى وقد عنت من كار فطم
حكما عليهم ولفطر هم
العسر قد ماتب والحسد بطل
ارحما فالت المفر حنا
ولمود الحسبد بالحففه ٥٥
والسمح لله دام
امنكم م

لس سمعه اللحي اللها لی
نسی في مصد الكتب المبارك العبد لحمقیره ٥٥ م شم تم

No. 445, with date of MS.
(*From a photograph by M. D. Gibson.*)

To face page ○○

كرز سمعان الصفا رئيس التلاميذ
من النسخة الموجودة فى دير طور سينا
المكتوبة فى سنة ١٨٣
من سنين العرب

# PRÆDICATIO PETRI.

بسم الاب والابن وروح القدس اله واحد هذا كرز سمعان
الصفا رييس التلاميذ ومتقدمهم بطرس حين بعثه المسيح ربنا
والاهنا يكرز برومية المدينة

دعا الله سمعان الصفا فقال له وكلمه سمعان سمعان رييس التلاميذ
رومية تريدك فاذهب اخرج الى هاولى القوم الذين قد اطغاهم 5
الشيطان فلما سمع ذلك سمعان تلميذ الاله اخذ يبكى بين يدى
الله ويقول الاهى اين اذهب وانا شيخ كبير وليس استطيع امشى
وليس لى ذهب ولا فضة ولا دابة فكيف اذهب اموت مثل الهالك
الذى يهلك اريد منك يا رب تغفر لى وتميتنى فى بيت المقدس
page 2 حيث كان امرك ثم اموت على كلمتك فقال الرب لسمعان لا 10
تجعل الفزع فى قلبك انى اعطيك سلطان الملك فلا تخاف اذهب
فادخل فيما بينهم فلا تخاف كلم المرضى فيبرون وقول للعمى
ابصروا فيبصرون فان لم يقبلوا ويمسكوا كلامك ويعلمون انى فى
السما فكلم الارض فتبتلعهم وكل شى ¹تربطه فى الارض انا اربطه
فى السما وكل شى تحله فى الارض انا احله فى السما انا فى 15
السما وانت فى الارض الغريبة تدعونى من بعيد فاجيبك عن

¹ Cod. ربطتوا.

قريب فقال سمعان الاهى لا تضيعنى انا عليك توكلت فان تتوانى

عنى فانى فى اسفل السافلين انحدر ثم ان سمعان قام الى اخوته

واصحابه ودموعه تجرى وقال قوموا يا اخوتى باجمعكم واذكروا

الحب الذى كان بيننا فاكثروا لى من الصلاة فى هذه الطريق

5 الذى قد اعطانى الله اياها فمثل الميت اخرج من عندكم فادعوا

لى فى صلواتكم فقالوا له اذهب بسلام يا قديس والله الذى فى

السما يكون معك واليمين الذى شقت البحر بين يدى بنى اسرايل

تكون معك يا قديس الله يا عمود الامانة اذهب فان ملاك الرب

يكون معك ويعينك على طريقك وعلى عدوك فجاز سمعان بطرس

10 البحر حتى بلغ مدينة رومية فاجمعوا حين راووه وبدوا يقولوا فيما

بينهم بحق ان هذا مسكين محتاج قد جا وهو مرجف وعيان

وعليه لباس خلق وبيننا مساكين كثيرة ومثل هذا لم نرى فوقع

حبيب الله على مزبلة انسان غنى وهو جيعان عطشان وقد اصابه

البرد وهو ملقى على وجهه بكثر ذكر الله فخرجت ابنة ذلك الغنى

15 فنظرت اليه ثم دخلت فقالت لابيها يا ابتاه ان شيخ مطروح على

مزبلتنا مثل العبد الكبير الذى لنا وهو فيما بيننا وفى جوف بيننا

فتدخله وتطعمه من الخبز الذى فى منزلنا فاجاب ابوها وقال لها

اذهبى يا حبيبتى كما قلتى يكون فحدى صلواته فخرجت الشابة

فسجدت له وقالت له قم ولا تبكى يا ابى فقد بلغت البيت فلا

20 تحزن قم وكل طعام واطرح الهم عنك فقام سمعان رييس

التلاميذ معها لكيما تقدم له طعام ياكل فوضعت له كرسى فجلس

وقدمت له انية فضة وذهب فسالها الما فذهبت بسرعة فجاات بقسط

ذهب فى يدها فحين دنت منه غطت يدها فقال لها سمعان قولى

لى يا شابة لاى شى غطيت يدك منى فقالت له كنت محصوبة

25 وقت دخولى على زوجى فلما اتى الزوج لياخذنى الى بيت اهله

وكان ¹الاكليل الذهب على راسى فاذا روانى الاسواق فلما بلغت

بيت زوجى ظهرنى هذا البرص عند ذلك استحيت اصحابتى

ورجعت الى بيت ابوية فانذرت نزرًا لالهتنا الاصنام واعطيت الكرا

page 6 الكبير وسجدت لكبارنا وهذا لى ستة اشهر منذ ظهر هذا الدا بى

٥ فلذلك استحيت وغطيت يدى ليلا تنظر اليها فاخذ بطوس ذلك

¹الكوز الما فصلى عليه بنية صادقه مقبولة روحانية ليسى فيها شى

من الجسدانى ثم اخذ بطرس ذلك ¹الكوز الما واعطاه للجارية

وقال لها اغسلى بدنك بهذا الما فلما غسلت بدنها بذلك الما بريت

وتنقت وصارت كانها لم ¹يصيبها شى قط من ذلك البرص الذى

١٠ كان بها ولما راات ذلك فزعت منه فزع شديد ثم انها اتت ابوها

وكان بواب فقالت له يا ابتاه ما يجلسك انظر الي فكشفت يدها

page 7 فلما راها ابوها قد اشتفت من ذلك البرص الذى كان ظهر بها

قال لها ويحك يا بنتى ما هذا الذى ارى بك اليوم قالت له بحق

اقول لك يا ابتاه ان الاه الحق دخل عندنا اليوم فنزل ابوها البواب

١٥ الى بطرس وقال له ابرى لى ما بقى من جسد ابنتى من هذا

البرص ¹وسالنى ما شيت من الذهب والفضة حتى اعطيك قال له

بطرس انا ابرى ما بقى من جسد ابنتك من هذا البرص وذهب

او فضة لا اريد منك بل اريد منك كلمة واحدة ان تومن بربى

يسوع المسيح وتترك عبادة الاصنام والشياطين الذى لا نعبد فقال

٢٠ page 8 البواب لبطرس لك ذلك عندى فقام بطرس فصب معمودية فى ذلك

الموضع الذى هم فيه فاخذ بطرس الجارية فعمدها فى تلك

المعمودية وطهوها بذلك الطهور وصبغها فى تلك المصبوغية بسم

الاب والابن وروح القدس فاستنقت من ذلك البرص الذى كان

بها كانه لم يخلق بها شى قط من ذلك البرص الذى كان بها

¹ Sic in Cod.

فلما راى ابوها البواب ذلك امن بالمسيح وترك عبادة الاصنام ثم

ان بطرس اقام عندهم يوم وليلة ثم بعد ذلك هوى بطرس ان

يخرج فى مدينة رومية ويظهر للناس فقال له البواب ان انت

ذهبت اليوم الى مدينة رومية لم تقدر تدخل وتدور فى اسواقها

5 فان لهم عيد ونذور ثم يذبحون فيها للاصنام فان راوك تدور

بينهم فى هذه الخلقان يقتلوك الالهة فقال بطرس للبواب الذى امن

بالمسيح لا بد لى ان اذهب الى مدينة رومية فان ربى المسيح

لمثل هذا اليوم ارسلنى ولامثال هذا ولا استطيع ان اعصى

ربى فانطلق بطرس حتى دخل مدينة رومية فاذا فيها كرازين

10 يكرزون ويقولون من كان من الناس فليلبس الحلل والثياب

والذهب والفضة والارجوان واللولو والا لا يلوم الا نفسه فالتفت

الشعوب واحبارهم الى بطرس كلما به فقالوا له ايها الشيخ الاحمق

اين تذهب اليوم بهذه الخلقان التى اراك اليوم عليك ان ملك

رومية قتلك من البس لبوس الذهب والفضة وتعال الى موضع الهتنا

15 فقال بطرس الملوك والاحبار والشعوب هذا اللباس لباس ربى الذى

اعطانى الذى لا اله غيره فانظروا ذلك القول وغضبوا من ذلك

غضبًا شديدا وتامروا على ان يرجموه بالحجارة لقوله فى المسيح

انه الاله فلما راى ذلك بطرس اتى الى موضع مشرق حيث كانت

الاهتمهم فتوحد ثم ¹يدعوا المسيح بنية صادقة مقبولة روحانية لم

20 تخالطها شيا من الجسدانية فى ذلك المقام فحيث خرج ملك

رومية وملوك كثيرة وشعوب واحبار الاف لا تحصى عدتهم ومعه

ماية جارية خمسين منهن متزوجات وخمسين لم يدخلن على

ازواجهن بعد وقد اُخذن وربطن للذبح نذرا لالهتهم الاصنام

والشياطين الذين كانوا يعبدون فلما راى ذلك بطرس رفع نظره

page 9
page 10
page 11

¹ Sic in Cod.

الى السما وقال ربى والاهى لا صبر لى بعد شى اراه ولكن رحمتك

وقدرتك فى مثل هذه الساعة احتاجها فاستجاب المسيح لبطرس

دعوته فبعث سحاب شديد وريح عاصف فالقيت تلك الاصنام

فتكسرت وخرجت منها شياطين واوت الجبال فلما راى ذلك ملك

page 12  رومية قال للجوارى اذهبن انتن الى [1]ابايكم وقال للخمسين 5

الناقية اذهبن انتن الى [1]بيوتكم فان ملكى قد فتى من تلك الظلمة

التى كانت على ذلك الشرف منها كان تخرج النار ومنها فتى

ملكى فى ذلك المقام حين اتاه الرسول من بيته يقول يا ملك

رومية ما تعردك وابنك وحبيبك قد مات فقال ملك رومية للملوك

والشعب والاحبار والالوف الذى لا تحصى عدتهم فانصرفوا معه 10

حتى اتوا منزله فخرجت امراته فقالت له يا ملك روميه اى شى

جلوسك وابنك وحبيبك قد مات تعال نبكى على وحيدنا اليوم

فجات ابنة البواب [1]الذى بريت من البرص فدخلت على ملك

page 13  رومية وقالت له يا ملك رومية ما يبكيك على وحيدك اليوم

ان فى المدينة شيخ ضعيف عليه خلقان ابعث اليه فهو يقيم 15

وحيدك هذا فقال لها ملك رومية يا جارية تستخزين بى الحجارة

تتكلم او العمى يبصرون او الموتى يقومون فكيف تقولين ان

وحيدى يقوم تعالى ابكى على وحيدى اليوم وجميع [1]اصحاباتك

فقالت له يا ملك روميه تعرفنى قال لها نعم انتى ابنة البواب

البرصا قالت له يا ملك رومية ليس انا [1]برصى وكشفت ساعدتها 20

ووجهها فلما نظر اليها قال لها ويحك يا جاريه ما هذا الذى اراك

page 14  فيه اليوم قالت له حقا اقول لك يا ملك رومية ان الشيخ الضعيف

المسكين الذى ذكرت لك هو الذى ابرانى وهو يقيم ابنك وحيدك

فى هذا اليوم فبعث الى الملوك والاحبار كلها فقال لهم اطلبوا

[1] Sic in Cod.

لهذا الشيخ الذى ذكرت هذه الجارية فطلبوا الملوك والاحبار
لبطرس حتى اصابوه فى المدينة بخلقانه فادخلوه على ملك رومية
فقال له ملك رومية ايها الشيخ ان اقمت ابنى ووحيدى فى
هذا اليوم فلك ملكى فقال له بطرس اما ابنك وحبيبك فانا اقيم

5 وملكك لا اريد اما اريد كلمة واحدة ان تعبد ربى والاهى يسوع
page 15
المسيح خالق السما والارض الذى لا اله غيره وتترك هذه الالهة
والاصنام الذى تعبد فقال له ملك رومية يا بطرس لك ذلك ان
اقمت ابنى فقال بطرس لملك رومية ابعث الى الملوك والشعوب
والاحبار من اهل مملكتك ممن داخل وخارج واجمعهم واحمل

10 ابنك هذا الميت على سريره وتعال الى موضع الهتك التى تعبد
فبعث ملك رومية الى جميع الملوك والاحبار والقواد وحمل ابنه
الوحيد بسريره فجا الى موضع الاصنام التى كانوا تعبدوها فتوحد
page 16
بطرس الى جانب السرير يدعوا الى المسيح ويقول ربى والاهى
انت الذى بعثتنى الى رومية لسلامة اهلها وخلاصهم وانت الذى

15 سببت موت هذا الخاطى لخلاص الجميع عند اقامتى اياه باسمك
فاظهر فى هذا الوقت قوتك بذكرى اسمك واسم ناسوتك فلما
قال هذا قام الميت ابن الملك من سريره حتى اتى الى بطرس
فسجد له وقال سلام عليك يا تلميذ المسيح سلام عليك يا
قديس الله سلام عليك يا من كاتب تكلمه الملايكة سلام عليك

20 يا من استجاب الملك دعوته حتى رجعت روحى الى جسدى
page 17
ثم التفت الميت الذى قام الى ابوه ملك رومية وقال الويل لك
يا ابتاه وما كنا نعبد الويل لك يا ابتاه واى خطايا كنا فيها الويل
لك يا ابتاه ان هذا الشيخ يدعوك الى الاه عظيم شديد القدرة
وان الملايكة تكلم هذا الشيخ تكليما الويل لك يا ابتاه فاى ظلمة

---

[1] Sic in Cod.

كنا فيها يامن الملك فى ذلك اليوم الوقت بالله وجميع الملوك
والاحبار وقال الملك لابنه اخبرنى بقصتك فقال له الغلام انى عند
ما خطفت صرت الى اقصى السما فلما صرت بين يدى كرسى
العزة كان هذا الشيخ واقف ثم يتضرع واجناد الملايكة وقوف وقال
الرب من كرسيه تقضى حاجة بطرس ريس كنيستى ومع هذا 5
الصوت رجعت نفسى الى جسدى فقال الملك لبطرس ايه السيد    page 18
امرنا بما شيت فقام بطرس فصب معمودية فى الموضع الذى كانت
الهتم فيه وعمد الملك وابنه وجميع باطارقته وجميع الاحبار والقواد
حتى كان بطرس لا يقوى ان يعمد الناس من كثرتهم حتى ان
بطرس كان ياخذ من ما المعمودية فيرش على الناس فمن كانت 10
تصيبه نقطة واحدة كان يعمد فامن جميع اهل رومية واقام فيها
بطرس يكرز ويعمد ويعلم وكان الناس يجوه من كل وجه
فيعمدون منه ويامنون بالمسيح ويتركون الدنيا ويهجرون الاهل    page 19
والمال ويطلبوا الامانة بالمسيح الذى له السبح من الان والى
دهو الداهرين امين والسبح لله دايما وعلينا رحمته امين ٠٠٠    15

# MARTYRIUM JACOBI.

هذه شهادة يعقوب بن حلفى وتمام جهاده فى تسعة ايام تشرين
الاول بسلام الرب امين

كــان لمــا دخل يعقوب مدينة اورشليم لينادى فيها بالانجيل
المقدس وكل العجايب [1]الاهوت لكيما كل من يسمع منه يامن
5 بالله بقلب نقى ويخلص نفسه ٠:٠ فاما يعقوب التلميذ ففكر فى
قلبه كيف تسمع منه الجماعة وتومن بالله وانه دخل الى الهيكل
حيث تجتمع فيه الجماعة فوجد جمعا كثيرا من اليهود مجتمعين ٠:٠
وانه ابتدا فى اوساطهم يبشرهم بفرح عظيم وابتهاج بين يدى
جماعتهم ٠:٠ واوسع القول وشرح الايمان بالله ٠:٠ فشهد على الوحيد
10 بن الله كلمة الحيوة اله كل الدهور يسوع المسيح انه هو بن
الله بالحقيقة وانه هو الكاين مع الاب قبل كل الدهور ٠:٠ هو فى
الاب والاب فيه هو الذى هو كلمة الاب ٠:٠ اذ قال نخلق انسانا بشبهتنا
وصورتنا وهو الساكن فى السما مع ابيه وهو على عرش الشاروبيم
والسارفيم تمجدوه ٠:٠ وهو الذى عـن يمين العظمة فى العلا ٠:٠ وهو
15 الحال فى بطن العذرى مريم ٠:٠ وهو الرب يسوع المسيح الذى
ولدته مارتمريم العذرى ٠:٠ وهو الاله الذى تانس ٠:٠ هذا اعتراف
التلميذ بين يدى تلك الجماعه بغير خوف مـن اخـرين الناس ٠:٠

[1] Sic in Cod.

شهد على ميلاد بن الله الوحيد وشهد بموته وقيامته من الاموات
وصعوده الى ابيه الذى فى السما ٠٠ وعلم جميع من حضر الامانة
بالمسيح ٠٠ فلما سمعت الجماعة ما قاله التلميذ غضبوا غضبا شديدا
الذى من ابيهم الشيطان الحال فيهم على تلميذ الرب يسوع
المسيح ٠٠ وتعاونوا كلهم وتقلدوا دمه جميع من حضر وسمع ٥
كلامه ٠٠ ومسكوا التلميذ المبارك وقدموه الى اقلوذيوس الملك
واقاموا عليه شهود زورا ٠٠ وقالوا للملك هذا الانسان مطغى ٠٠
يطوف البلاد والمدن ويقول انا عبد يسوع المسيح ٠٠ ويمنعهم من
طاعة الملك ٠٠ فلما سمع الملك هذا من اجل التلميذ المبارك امر
ان يرجم بالحجارة حتى يموت ٠٠ وان اليهود لعنهم الله رجموه ١٠
كما امر الملك ٠٠ وهكذى كانت شهادة التلميذ يعقوب بن حلفى
اخو مثى فى تسعة ايام من شهر ¹تشير الاول ٠٠ وقبر عند الهيكل
فى اورشليم والسبح لله دايما ابدا

¹ Sic in Cod.

# PRÆDICATIO SIMONIS.

هـذه بشارة الطوبان القديس سيمن بـن كلاوبا الذى يدعى
يهوذا الذى نفسيره ناثانايل الذى يدعى الغيور وصار اسقف فى
اورشليم بعد يعقوب اخو الرب يسوع المسيح

كان حين اجتمعوا التلاميذ على طور الزيتون ليقتسموا مدن
5 العالم كلها ٠:٠ وفيما همر يصلوا ويباركوا الله جل اسمه اذ حضر
الرب يسوع المسيح فى وسطهم ٠:٠ فقال لهـم سلام ابى يحل
عليكم يا تلاميذى الاطهار ٠:٠ وانهم تساهموا فخرج سهر يهوذا
الجليلى الى بلاد السامرية ٠:٠ وان ينادى فيهم بانجيل الرب يسوع
المسيح ٠:٠ اجاب سيمن فقال للرب يكون معنا يا سيدنا فى كل
10 موضع نحل فيه ٠:٠ ونحن نصبر على جميع ما يحل بنا ٠:٠ لكن
يخرج معى ابى بطرس لكى ان يوصلنى الى ارض السامرية ٠:٠ قال
له الرب السهر الذى لبطرس ان يخرج الى رومية لينادى فيها ٠:٠
ولكن هو يخرج معك حتى يوصلك بسلام ٠:٠ واقول لك انه من
بعد بشارتك فنداك فيهم انت تعود الى اورشليم بعد موت يعقوب
15 الصديق وتكون فيها اسقف من بعده ٠:٠ وانت تتمر جهادك مثل ما
تمر يعقوب الصديق فى ذلك الموضع ٠:٠ فالان يا صفى سيمن اخرج
بسلام قوة ابى يصحبك ٠:٠ وبارك عليه الرب هو وجميع التلاميذ ٠:٠
وصعد الى السما بمجد عظيم ٠:٠ وبعد صعود الرب الى السما قام

سيمن وصلى وانحدر الى اورشليم ومعه بطرس وسار الى السامرية ::

ونادى فيهم ببشرى الانجيل :: وان سيمن التلميذ دخل الى وسط

مجمعهم ونادى فيهم باسم يسوع المسيح :: فلما سمعوا اليهود

الساكنين فى ذلك الموضع قاموا عليه وضربوه ضربا وجيعا وزجوا

به الى خارج المدينة :: وان بطرس قبله وودعه :: وان سيمن عاد ٥

وقام فى مجمعهم ثلثه ايام ينادى فيهم باسم يسوع المسيح ::

فامن منهم قوم ومنهم قوم لم يومنوا :: وفى اخر اليوم الثالث اعتل

بن ريس الجماعة :: وكان اسمه يعقوب ومات :: وان رجلا ممن

امن بما كان سيمن يقول حضر الى والد الصبى الميت وقال

له هوذا تلميذ المسيح هاهنا ادعوه يصلى على الصبى :: فمضى ١٠

الرجل مسرعا ودعا تلميذ سيدنا المسيح فحضر بفرح ووقف على

الغلام الميت وقال لوالد الغلام الذى مات تومن بالذى صلب انه

هو بن الله :: عند ذلك ترى مجد الله :: قال له ابو الغلام ان

قام ابنى من الموت حتى انظره حى انا اومن بيسوع المصلوب page 3

انه بن الله الحي وان التلميذ عاد بوجهه الى المشرق وصلى وقال ١٥

سيدى يسوع المسيح الذى صلب على عهد بلاطس البنطى انت

اهلتنى لهذه الخدمة ان انادى باسمك المبارك ولانك تجسمت هذا

من اجلنا لتنقذنا من يد ١العدوا :: انظر الى هذا الغلام الميت

وبارادتك فامره ان يقوم لكيما يمجد اسمك اليوم فى وسط جماعة

هذه المدينة ليومنوا باسمك المقدس :: فلما قال سيمن التلميذ ٢٠

المبارك هذا عاد الى الموضع الذى فيه الغلام الميت وقال باسم

الاب والابن وروح القدس يقوم ينهض حى وتكون سالم لكيما

كلمن حضر يومن باسم سيدى يسوع المسيح :: وفى تلك الساعة

فتح الغلام عينيه وقام وجلس وامر ان يقدم اليه ما ياكل ::

فلما نظروا الجماعة هذا العجب تقدموا كلهم وسجدوا فى الارض

للتلميذ وامنوا كلهم بالله وهم قايلين واحد هو اله سيمن تلميذ

يسوع المسيح نومن بيسوع المسيح انه بن الله الحي وان ابوى

الغلام طرحا نفوسهما على رجلى التلميذ وقالا يا سيدنا كيف

5 نخلص قال لهما تومنا من كل قلوبكما فانتما تخلصا ٠٠ وانه

page 4 وعظهم من الكتب المقدسة وعمدهم باسم الاب والابن وروح القدس

واء 'اهم السراير المقدسة ٠٠ وامرهم ان يبنوا البيعة وقسم لهم اسقف

الذى كان ريس الجماعة واسمه قرنيليوس ٠٠ وقسم لهم قسوسا

وشماسة واعطاهم الانجيل المقدس ٠٠ واقام عندهم شهرا يعلمهم

10 كلام الله وبعد ذلك رجع الى اورشليم فلما قتلوا اليهود يعقوب

كانوا التلاميذ مجتمعين فى اورشليم ٠٠ مسكوا سيمن وجعلوه اسقفا

باورشليم ٠٠ وكان يعلمهم كلام الله ويعرفهم ما فى الانجيل

وخلاص نفوسهم وان اليهود كانوا غضابى عليه وكان فى اورشليم

يسبح الرب يسوع المسيح فى كل الاوقات والاحيان وله ذلك

15 الى دهر الداهرين امين

# MARTYRIUM SIMONIS.

هذه شهادة سيمن بن كلاوبا تلميذ الرب يسوع المسيح تم
جهاده فى عشرة ايام من شهر ايار يسالم الرب امين

كان بعد نياحة يعقوب الصديق جعل سيمن بن كلاوبا
الذى يدعى يهوذا اسقف اورشليم ؛؛ وعاش ماية وعشرين سنة ؛؛
وقال فى اخر عمره اريد ان يهراق دمى على اسم الرب يسوع 5
المسيح ؛؛ وانه بنى كنايسا فى كل موضع باورشليم ؛؛ وقسم لهم
page 5 قسوس وشماسة والكنيسة الاولة التى بناها باسم الرب يسوع المسيح ؛؛
والثانية باسم العذرى مريم والدة الرب على الارض ؛؛ ابعد جنس
البشر من عبادة الشيطان واهلهم لملكوته ؛؛ والثالثة سماها باسم
ميخايل رييس الملايكة الذى هو شفيع لجنس البشر حتى رجع عنهم 10
الرجز وحلت عليهم الرحمة ؛؛ والرابعة سماها باسم التلاميذ ؛؛ وكان
حريص ان يعطل امانة اليهود وعبادتهم الدنسة ومجمعهم الشرير ؛؛ فانه
كان يجلس يعظ كل واحد كلام الله حتى عمر الكنايس التى
بناها وان معرفة الله ظهرت لكل الناس من الكبير الى الصغير
والرجال والنسا ؛؛ فامنوا كلهم على يدى التلميذ حتى ان اهل 15
المدينة تركوا مجمع اليهود وتبعوا الحق الذى علمهم اياه التلميذ
من قبل الرب يسوع ؛؛ فاما اليهود فلما سمعوا فعل التلميذ
المبارك وانه يريد يعطل دينهم ومبعودهم اجتمعوا كلهم الكبير

والصغير وتشاوروا جميعا على التلميذ ليقتلوه انه فاعل الشر ∻

[1]وهكذى تجمعوا عليه اليهود كلهم بغضب وحرد وقيدوه واسلموه

الى درايانوس الملك وتشاهدوا عليه باجمعهم عند الملك وقالوا له

page 6 اسمع منا نعرفك ما يفعل هذا هو ساحر ∻ وان الملك فى جميع

5 ما قالوا غضب شديدا على التلميذ وقال له لك اقول يا فاعل

الشر قيل لى انك ساحر تسحر كلمن فى هذه المدينة ∻ قال له

التلميذ لسمع منى ايه الملك الذى لَيس له عقل ولا حاسة ليس

انا ساحر ولا اعرف كيف يعمل صنعة السحر ∻ بل انا عبد لسيدى

يسوع المسيح اله كل الخليقة وملك الملوك الله العظيم القادر

10 الذى يهلك كل الهة الامم ∻ فلما سمع الملك هذا الكلام من

التلميذ غضب غضبا شديدا وسلمه الى قوم اشرار ليصلبوه وان

اليهود يجعموا عليه واخرجوا التلميذ المبارك سيمن بن كلاوبا

ليصلب [1]كاامر الملك المنافق وعلقوه على الصليب وعذبوه حتى

تنيح وتم شهادته فى عشرة ايام من شهر ايار ولله ماسك الكل

15 المجد والكرامة الى دهر الداهرين امين ∻

[1] Sic in Cod.

www.ingramcontent.com/pod-product-compliance
Ingram Content Group UK Ltd.
Pitfield, Milton Keynes, MK11 3LW, UK
UKHW012021280225
455719UK00011B/430